POEMS ABOUT PEOPLE

ROBIN YOUNG GOZA
AND FAMILY

WESTBOW
PRESS®
A DIVISION OF THOMAS NELSON
& ZONDERVAN

WestBow Press books may be ordered through booksellers or by contacting:

WestBow Press
A Division of Thomas Nelson & Zondervan
1663 Liberty Drive
Bloomington, IN 47403
www.westbowpress.com
844-714-3454

ISBN: 979-8-3850-1973-1 (sc)
ISBN: 979-8-3850-1974-8 (e)

Library of Congress Control Number: 2024903998

Print information available on the last page.

WestBow Press rev. date: 6/6/2024

Dedication

. . . .

This collection of poems is dedicated to all of my family and friends who gave me the inspiration for most of the poems, which made this book possible.

After looking through stock photos, I realized that what I really wanted on the cover was pictures of my family. I decided to draw the illustrations myself. If my family members see an image on the cover that looks like them, and they like it, it is definitely a drawing of them. If they see an image on the cover that looks a little like them, but they don't like it, it isn't them. Please understand that some of the reference photos that I used to draw the images were from different decades. If you don't see yourself, I'm sorry. Either I couldn't find a picture of you that I thought that I could draw, or I had finally passed the point with drawing that I was just done. It reminded me of what Mom did with her kids for much of our childhood. She would start to shout to get the attention of one of her nine children, "Sha...Cher...Ste...." Then she would just give up on figuring out the name and yell, "You! Get over here and start your chores," (or whatever it was that she wanted us to do). She didn't feel like thinking anymore, and neither did I.

I'm so glad to have you in my life. Thank you all for being my beautiful family.

Preface

The poems I have included are about family, friends, people I have observed, our faith, and my own experiences. In most cases, I have removed or changed names. The people in some poems may be composites of more than one person. The significance is not that I (or these other particular people) experienced these feelings, actions, or major events. What is important is that many other people have encountered these same or similar incidents and have felt these emotions as well. When your children or parents almost drive you up the wall, or when you have been bullied, abused, frustrated, depressed, or have known overwhelming grief, be aware that you are not the only one. Others have been there before and have made it through the trials.

However, I also write about amusing, joyful, and sometimes exhilarating experiences, like those involving my children or grandchildren. Whether happy or hurting, concerned or consumed, describing details or displaying the big picture, I have tried to keep my sense of humor intact. God has used humor with me numerous times, and I assume He knows that humor heals a heavy heart. Plus, a good laugh is fun and can make you feel better. I have even included some short poems about children that are easy to create and make the child feel special. You could give it a try, too.

Moreover, I have realized that we all need more grace than we usually get from others and even from ourselves. Thankfully, God easily dispenses grace to His children, as well as mercy and love. Take the time to be more gracious. As someone else once said, "You may be the only Jesus that someone sees." Reflect Him well.

My husband and I share five children (and their spouses), fifteen grandchildren, and nine great-grandchildren. They provide plenty to write about.

I am one of nine children: three girls and six boys. I don't know how Mom did it.

Additionally, my father died in 2015, one of my younger brothers in 2020, and my mother in 2022. Both Dad and Mom had dementia. I have known heartache and grief.

I have loved writing for a long time, but started doing it more regularly as a young adult.

The last chapter includes poems by other family members and information about them.

Robin Young Goza

Acknowledgements

I wish to thank both of my daughters, Stephanie Gray and Kimberly Kuchar, for reading most of my poems and giving me numerous suggestions for improving them. My younger daughter, Kimberly, previously helped me proof and edit some of my favorite poems when I struggled to find the right words to express precisely what I was trying to say. Her vast vocabulary and writing skills never cease to amaze me. She also read through a draft of this manuscript and suggested some changes.

I am also grateful for the last-minute efforts of my friend Linda Young (also my sister-in-law) in helping me get my poems ready for submission. She read all of the poems, made suggestions, and then read my submission information answers. She helped me find the peace of mind I needed.

Years ago, I was talking with my dad about combining some of my poems into a book, and together we came up with several titles, which led to the one I have now. Thanks, Dad, for your clarity of thought.

Robin, a.k.a. Mom

Contents

· ·

1. God's Love

A Different Night before Christmas and More 1
Living for Him 3
The Great Commission 5
Can You Answer My Question? 7
What Is Your Part? 8
Mere Mortals May Meet Their Maker 10
My Other Dad 12

2. God's Leaders

God's Pastor 17
The Joy of Leading Worship 18

3. Love and Relationships

Couples Then, Couples Now 21
Marrying Their Kin 24
Prenuptial Agreement 26
A Special Strength 27
My Gift to You 28
It's Your Birthday. Celebrate! 29
To My Valentine 30
For My Valentine 32
A Valentine Wish 32
A Father's Day Poem 33
Twenty Years 34
A Blessing for Our Daughter on Her Wedding Day 36
Darts 37
Judging Beauty, Judging People 40
Can I Give It to Him? 42
Our Nights before Christmas 43

4. Parents

What Is a Dad? 47
Father 48
Dads and Daughters 49

Different Points of View 50

The Inspiring, Inimitable, Knowledgeable, Noble Nonagenarian 51

To Mom for Mother's Day 52

The Legacy 54

The Right Hairstyle 56

Fixating on Figures or Faces? 58

What Happened to My Mom? 60

Maturing versus Aging 62

Christmas Time at My House 64

5. Children and Grandchildren

Thirteen! 71

Thirteen! 72

Happy Belated Birthday, Daughter 74

Our Grandson 75

Katie 76

Our Grandson at Fourteen 77

Our Princess 80

Twelve on the Twelfth and Tenaciously Testing as a Teen Prematurely 81

My Talented Grandson 84

Terri 86

Patti 87

My Grandson Is Eighteen! 90

A Birthday Wish 91

Waiting for Wonky Weather 92

Lacie 93

A Birthday Poem 95

Welcome to Our Family 96

Your Lives 98

The Son 99

The Plan 104

Words Beat Sticks and Stones 105

The Perfect Picture 106

Learning to Be a Man 109

Teaching Our Boys to Be Men 111

6. Fun Poems for Our Children to Feel Special

A Valentine for My Daughter 117

Emily 118

My Daughter 118

A Song for Karen 118

A School Prayer 118
M O N I Q U E – an acrostic poem 119
L I D I A – an acrostic poem 119
R O G E R – an acrostic poem 119
Belle 120
Davis 120
Ezer 120

7.   Friendships

Ellie and Her Friends 123
A Belated Valentine for Ellie 126
A New Friend 127
A Masked Woman No More 128
Walking in Her Shoes 129
Leticia, a Faithful Friend 131
Gather to Learn and Encourage 134

8.   Changes

Is My Brain Trying to Rebel? 139
Words 140
Getting Older 141
Allergies and Asthma Are Atrocious! 142
Turning 30 Ain't So Bad 143
Phantom Phun on Phantom Horse 144

9.   Grief: My Daddy's and Best Friend's Deaths

Praying to My Father for My Dad 147
My Daddy 148
My Dad's Salvation 151
Father God, HELP! Sometimes Grief Just Stinks 153
When You're in a Fog, Look to the Light 155
My Grief Journey—Jolts, Justice, and Just Plain Awesome! ... 158
Alone, or Not? 161

10.   Grief: My Younger Brother Steve's Death

Wanted: Good Assistant for Mr. Young 165
The Many Faces of Steve 166
My Grief Is Not Always Friendly 170
I Don't Want the Pain 172
Grief Can Hurt 174

Dispelling the Darkness 176
Depression and Its Abuse 177
Our Grief Facilitators 179

11. Grief: My Mom's Death

A Mom's Love 183
Dear Husband... 188
Mom's Death, My Reactions.. 189
Family 190
The Notebook Lesson 192
My Tears 194
Mom and Me 196

12. Our Legacy—a Family's Faith, Love for Learning, and Penning of Poetry

1857 – 1895 205
The Soldier and the Quilt.. 207
"In memory of the dead" 209
In Memoriam 211
Santa's Disappointment.. 213
Billy and the Crane... 216
Motherhood 217
The Patriarch 218
The Present... 219
Mr. Young's Assistant 220
A Wife Is Like Fine Crystal.. 222
The Hidden Treasure 223
Momma, ... 224
A Mother's the Best Friend a Daughter Can Have............................ 225
Mother 226
Ode to Max 227
Mazda... 228
Mazda, Our New "Little Boy" 229

—— 1 ——

God's Love

A Different Night before Christmas and More

'Twas the night before Christmas, when all through the town
People rushed to find shelter, find rest and lie down.
The innkeeper's wife had just locked the front door.
They were crowded already, didn't want any more.

The groups were complaining about a new tax,
While she and her husband had been breaking their backs.
The census was horrid; now they'd know where you lived.
What if you had no money, nothing left you could give?

Would they care of the illness your child's had so long,
Your husband's sickness or death? How'd it all go so wrong?
These thoughts and these burdens were spoken aloud,
When they all came together as the inn's noisy crowd.

Walking slowly through town was a man and his wife.
She looked young and quite burdened, soon to birth a new life.
They cared less of the census and more of their goal.
Mary soon would deliver One who'd make all men whole.

The Scriptures had said it, so they knew it was true.
God's angel confirmed it. What were they now to do?
How does one poor and humble raise a man to be king?
All she did was say, "Yes!" What would their future bring?

A new baby, so helpless, asleep on the hay,
Didn't look like the leader that He must be some day.
About a week later to the temple they went.
Anna knew who the child was, knew He was Heaven-sent.

Simeon was another who acknowledged the boy.
Being in the lad's presence brought them both such great joy.
As she did with the visits from both shepherds and kings,
Mary pondered it all, her heart full of these things.

The three stayed in town until God let them know
It was no longer safe; to Egypt they must go.
Obedient then, as they had been before,
They kept the child safe until God called once more.

The young boy grew up; His mission began.
He taught of God's love, salvation for man.
Then He paid the full price for the sins of us all
As He hung on the cross, on the hill of the skull.

But it didn't end there; after death He arose
And instructed His men to take His message to those
Around the whole world, till they get to the end—
All should know of His love, every nation of men.

God loves us, though sinners, spiritually dead.
Now all we must do is believe what He said:
His Son died for our sins. He took our place.
The penalty's paid; He offers us grace.

We should accept His free gift; that's all we must do.
He has mansions in Heaven now waiting, it's true.
Faith in His Son is what sets us free.
We can't earn salvation with all our good deeds.

But we also won't lose this new gift when we're *bad*,
For He loves us too much. He's not that kind of dad.
Once we're part of His family, we're in it to stay.
We don't make the rules; we must do it His way.

As Mary said, "Yes," we, too, must decide.
Do we believe His Son came and for us He died?
On the night before Christmas, do you think of His Son?
As you walk through your town, do you believe what He's done?

Living for Him

My friend has been misunderstood
By those who ought to know
She has desires as others do,
But her behavior tries to show:

Her heart belongs to someone who
Has loved her all her life.
He surrounds her with forever love;
Others live with mostly strife.

While the world goes after what it wants,
She waits for her Father's plan.
Others cannot comprehend
Why she seems "prudish" with her man.

Her daddy was a preacher
Who taught of mercy and of grace,
So it's hard when pushy people
Get right up in her face.

It makes her sad or sometimes mad.
She knows it isn't right,
But she must follow Christ's example
Every day and every night.

Responding to aggressive people
Is not an easy task,
But the Lord, the worlds' creator,
Knows behavior that attracts.

"Do to others as you'd have them do"
Appears as nonsense to most men.
They like to do before others do,
To have treasures in the end.

Living "in the world, not of the world"
Is what our Lord still asks,
But when we're in pain, wonderin' what to do,
It's an overwhelming task.

Jesus says to let his light shine through,
Love others with His love.
Some see Jesus only through our acts.
Our Father smiles on us above.

My friend may know some just don't get
Why she acts the ways she does,
But she'll keep on doin' what Jesus says
And sharing her Father's love.

The Great Commission

....

The Great Commission Jesus gave
Seemed for the men around
Him as He spread His Dad's Good News,
While going town to town.

But Jesus saw it differently.
His followers He sent out,
Sometimes the twelve, once seventy,
With instructions not to doubt.

He gave them power to perform
Signs and wonders for the lost.
He warned them some would hate them too,
But each soul was worth the cost.

I've come to realize, recently,
His ways are not our ways,
For he used a lady, wheelchair bound,
Who roamed the halls most days.

She had always been an extrovert,
Who liked people, their attention.
When her fading memory made it hard
To converse, to reduce her tension,

God helped her find a question
She could ask most anyone,
"Are you a Christian? Do you believe?"
She knew the topic. It was fun.

God accepts the gifts we offer Him,
Even if they may seem small.
He empowers the weak to tell of Him.
He loves to use us all.

We know of a little drummer boy
Who played music for a king,
Who was a baby at the time.
The boy gave his everything.

The lady had three girls, six boys,
But no longer knew their names.
Her sense of humor and love for God
Were what seemed to keep her sane.

The Helpers at the Memory Care Home
Where Mom lived her last years
Loved working with her, laughed with her.
Her death brought them to tears.

This woman in her nineties,
With memories mostly gone,
Still told those who would listen:
God would someday take her Home.

Is the Great Commission Jesus gave
For church leaders and the trained,
Or does He want us all to share
Till the whole world knows His name?

I know what Mama thought!

Can You Answer My Question?

(written while I was in high school)

Why do they all just laugh and scoff
When I start to talk about God?
They and the good Lord's enemy
Are perhaps two peas in a pod?

Why do they think it's awful,
When someone's deriding Him,
For me to stand and say he's wrong
And show my belief in Him?

Why do they think I'm terrible,
Because I mention the Lord?
Is it because I have some hope
And might not fall with the horde?

If someone could answer my question
And won't just scoff and scorn,
Perhaps with some of the good Lord's help
Both of us could learn.

What Is Your Part?

I was talking with a friend,
Showing poems that I wrote.
She said she couldn't do it if she tried.

I proceeded to remind her
Of her skills I don't possess,
Organizing VBS and teaching it worldwide.

We agreed that if we all
Had the same ideas and skills,
Our world would soon be boring, filled with strife.

God made each of us unique
Our looks, the languages we speak.
Our different passions, when engaged, enrich each life.

I remembered how the Bible
Said we're the hands and feet of Christ.
He's the head and we're the body by God's plan.

If we were all heads, we might roll,
But I don't think we'd have control
We'd look like the soccer ball, and not the man.

If we decided to be feet,
We could move in all directions,
But without a brain, would we know where to go?

If we were arms, we could all reach
To make things, take what we wish,
But would right and wrong be concepts we would know?

As you can see, we'd be a mess.
Perhaps our Lord knows what is best.
We do better when each person does his part.

We can each do it our way
Perform the part that we decide.
But we could never please our God without a heart.

The heart is where our Savior dwells.
Many Bible stories tell
How He knocks on our heart's door to let Him in.

He has given us free will.
It's our choice; He waits until
We accept His gift, His Way to be with Him.

Mere Mortals May Meet Their Maker

We've acknowledged mortality loiters:
Covid's an awful disease.
Our strength was so zapped;
My lungs filled up fast;
His blood pressure swiftly increased.

The Enemy hates God's children,
But he kills others as well.
He prides himself
On his cunning deceit,
Sending all he can to Hell.

God made men and angels and gave us free will,
Knowing some would choose wrong, not right.
Even angels who lived
In the presence of God
Chose the Angel of Darkness (once Light).

The rebels were cast down from Heaven to earth.
They began to corrupt God's creation.
They use half-truths and lies
And all means of disguise
To bring evil into every nation.

Even God's chosen people
Weren't immune to the sins.
A young man had pride;
His brothers then lied.
The youth was sold by these jealous men.

God used the youth to save the lives
Of men He chose for His own,
But in the desert
They made no effort
To worship God. They griped and moaned.

A wise young king built a holy temple
For men to worship their Holy God there.
But they wrote laws
And craved applause,
And killed God's Son without even a care.

Since Jesus's death we've had preachers
Who speak the truth to save men's souls.
Even in His time
False teachers lied.
Still faith in God's gift makes men whole.

Some family members have lived to a hundred,
Others eighty or even ninety.
Our race still we run
Till He tells us, "Well done."
Knowing life's been set by our Father Almighty.

I'm not looking for Death. I know it's out there,
But it's powerless without God's direction.
I'll keep telling my story
As it brings God the glory.
He watched over me before our connection.

As a young child I knew that God must be real.
My father and mother believed.
They were honest, showed love
To their family and others.
A loving Father wasn't hard to perceive.

For some reason I misunderstood how God loved.
He'd hear prayers, answer some, live in Heaven.
Before I speak to God now,
I clear space on my couch.
His Holy Spirit speaks with me where I'm livin.'

(The day I realized that Christianity is not just another religion, but a relationship with my Heavenly Father is the day my life changed forever! Thank you Abba, my Divine Daddy.)

My Other Dad

Lord, I know you're always there.
Help me stop and be aware.
And be more thankful in my prayers.

I love to sense you by my side.
I'm awed you'd care to so abide.
I felt your warm hug once; I cried.

You never leave or forsake your child.
I learned that once when I was riled,
While learning to tube-feed my child.

I couldn't put the tubes in right,
Had trouble going to sleep that night,
Until you said it'd be alright.

Your peace enveloped me; I slept.
Next day you showed I'm not inept.
I learned the skills, and then I wept.

I love to speak with my own dad,
But his dementia makes me sad,
Knowing the memory that he once had.

His unconditional love for me
Made it easy for me to see
The God of Heaven could really love me.

Your love amazes me each day.
Help me to listen when I pray.
Communication should be two-way.

It's hard to quiet my mind each day,
To hear you speak in your still, small way,
So I visualize our meeting in another way

My dad doesn't talk much, but when he speaks,
It's important: we listen; what might he teach?
So, though others may think it's quite a reach,

I imagine I'm sitting with my other Dad.
Being with each other makes us glad.
We speak; we listen. He's my Dad!

2

God's Leaders

God's Pastor

Our pastor is a man of God,
Who fully loves the Lord.
He speaks the truth, not words approved
By false leaders of the world.

He says to seek the Lord's desires,
Not what the world demands.
We're preparing for our final home.
We are pilgrims in this land.

Pastor warns against the world's desires.
Jesus points us to His Dad.
Loving others as we love our God
Gives us joy; evil makes some *mad*.

Pastor Ron reminds us
To trust in God's commands.
He suggests we put God's armor on,
Make sure our posts are manned.

Evil men have killed God's chosen ones
Since sibling envy shed pure blood.
Cain was marked to wander aimlessly.
Sin increased. God sent the flood.

Our real battle is a spiritual one,
Though we can see what evil's done.
While God's leading Ron to show the truth,
We read the Book; we know we've won.

Pastor warns that there are many signs
Pointing to this world's demise,
We must trust the Lord; no need to fear.
He'll be returning in the skies.

God's trained our pastor as He pleased,
For He knows the path he'll take.
He's musician, leader, preacher, friend.
He's here now for our church's sake.

17

The Joy of Leading Worship

He leads the worship Sunday morn;
His love for God abounds.
He takes the psalmist at his word
And makes a joyful sound.

He barely can contain himself;
His enthusiasm grows.
He moves around as he leads the choir.
God's love moves to his toes.

His wife stands there beside him
And lifts her clear strong voice.
Together with the band and choir
They help the church rejoice.

We thank God that we have this pair.
They're a gift from God above,
For they display to all His body
How to worship Him with love.

3

Love and Relationships

Couples Then, Couples Now

When God created Adam,
He started with just one.
Though God walked with His man each day,
He knew He wasn't done.

God caused His man to slumber
And then removed a bone
From which He made a woman.
Man should not be alone.

God woke the man from his deep sleep
And showed him his new gift.
The two, together, walked with God,
Until they caused a rift.

The serpent told the naïve girl
She should eat from the tree.
She ate, then shared with Adam.
They lived, but they could "see."

Their nakedness then caused them shame.
What they'd done wasn't right.
When God showed up to walk with them,
They hid, unnerved with fright.

He told them not to eat the fruit
From just that lonely tree.
All other food was theirs to eat,
But gods they thought they'd be.

Their sin had separated
Them from their holy God.
They did die when they ate the fruit:
Their spirits, not their bods.

We wish they hadn't eaten
From that forbidden tree.
Then we'd still have the garden,
Paradise for you and me.

The serpent lied; he always has.
He wanted to cause strife.
When God asked why the man ate there,
He promptly blamed his wife.

She wasn't guiltless, as we know,
For she then blamed the snake.
Their disobedience, blaming others,
Was more than God could take.

The first couple set a precedent
We've followed over time.
We shirk responsibility
For almost every crime.

The Father God was holy,
Could not ignore their sin.
He closed their lovely garden,
Would not let them back in.

They wandered, looking for a home,
As couples still must do.
If they had done as they were told,
They would not have been so blue.

They had to work hard for their food,
For God had cursed the ground.
If they had listened to their Dad,
He would still be around.

But would we really do it right,
Or do as they had done?
They may have been the first to sin,
But they're not the only ones.

We often put ourselves first,
And mate and children next.
If they don't do things as we want,
We get especially vexed.

Why must we emulate those two
And not walk with our Dad?
If He's not our priority,
We'll soon wish that we had.

He tells us how to really love
Our family and our friends.
He sent His Son to die for us
To walk with Him, again.

Marrying Their Kin

The pretty young girl saw the handsome young man
In his military clothes.
He didn't cuss, yell, drink, or smoke,
So he's the one she chose.

When she met his family, she was shocked.
The girls weren't what she'd visualized.
Instead of the closeness she had sought,
The warmth hoped for felt like ice.

Her hurt turned to anger; she wasn't amused.
Why did they treat her this way?
Resentment and bitterness grew in her heart
And remain there till today.

She loves to tell how they treated her wrong,
How he always took their side.
She can't see he's changed in 65 years,
Or that most of the culprits have died.

She wants all her children to love God, like her,
But she doesn't see their plight.
They don't see God's love pouring out,
But the desire to pick a good fight.

She tells everyone that her husband won't talk,
But she seldom stops for a breath.
He's silent while thinking about what he'll say,
So she speaks; she just can't resist.

She likes to converse with whoever will listen.
She tells them a joke or two,
But she's forgotten that conversation's two-way,
So she sleeps when she "listens" to you.

Her grown children love her, but don't understand
Why she treats them like kids to this day.
It could go back to the love from her folks
Or the "chill" from his kin that first day.

Her daddy worked nights and slept during the day,
So she didn't dare wake him up.
If she and her friends would make too much noise,
He would come out and yell and cuss.

Other times he worked months in towns far away,
He would go where the jobs were at.
Children don't understand why a parent must leave.
Did he love her, and would he come back?

Her mom also worked, so she wasn't home much,
And when she was home she was tired.
The young girl wondered if she really was loved
Or dressed up, shown off, and admired.

The mom spent her spare time with music and choir
And in genealogical cliques.
She would take her child shopping or out to a show
And sew her curtains or pretty outfits.

The girl and a young aunt grew up and helped out;
They shopped, cooked meals, and cleaned.
After schoolwork was done, they'd play cards or sing songs.
Was this all to love, what she's seen?

The handsome young man saw the pretty young girl,
Her lips, her hair, her eyes.
He desired to be with her and make her his own,
But neither realized

When you marry a person, you marry their kin.
In that you have no say.
So if you are smart, you will meet them all
Before your wedding day.

Prenuptial Agreement

What's mine is yours.
What's yours is mine.
That's how it should be.
Now I can share my debt with you,
And you share yours with me.

Now I can share my children,
And you can share yours too,
With all the fun and all the tears
They'll give to me and you.

Grandchildren are so special.
I get yours without fail,
No matter if they hug and kiss
Or jump and scream and yell.

I'll share with you bad habits.
I'll also share the good.
We couldn't do it differently,
Even though we should.

What's mine is yours.
What's yours is mine.
That's how it should be.
I want to share my life with you,
And you share yours with me.

A Special Strength

There's something special about the man I love
That sets him above all the others.
I sensed it when I first spoke to him on the phone.
I saw it when he spoke to me that very first time.
He seemed so different from so many men—
When he spoke with such sensitivity about his son and daughters,
And especially when he mentioned his grandchildren.
As impressed as I was with his love for his family,
The more he said, the more I thirsted to hear what he would say next.
Spiritually, he was a giant.
His relationship with the Lord surpassed all I had seen before.
He was shy, but outspoken, on certain subjects.
He had a strength I had never seen or felt or experienced before—
Strength of character, strength of convictions,
As well as pure physical strength.
He was the "gentle giant," sensitive, strong, special.
The second time I saw him, he showed up in shorts.
I was sunk!
His shyness, sensitivity, spirituality, and strength
Were only secondary to his sensuality.
I was sure he was sent from the Son Himself.
Who else would know what I really needed?
Nevertheless, as we sort through our sets of baggage, ,
I often have to smile through my tears at the Lord's sense of humor.
He must have laughed out loud as He set us in the same place,
Knowing that his two precious children
Would butt heads to knock off the rough spots
And put each other under such pressure
That someday soon they would shine again for Him as diamonds.
Diamonds shine brilliantly as nearby light reflects its inner beauty.
Diamonds are admired for their beauty and strength,
And so is my love.
His strength helps me feel safe as I snuggle softly beside him.
As we feel safe in our fathers' (and Father's) arms,
So I feel close beside my love.

My Gift to You

If I could buy you anything
With no concern for money,
You'd have a house beside a lake
Where we could sail, my honey.

You'd have a TV, large and flat,
With pictures like 3D,
Or a monitor for your work desk
Of the same good quality.

You'd have a grill to barbecue
That wouldn't burn the meat,
With all of the accessories
And a gauge to check the heat.

Perhaps we could go on a trip:
See Colorado mountains,
Or beaches while we're on a cruise,
Or far exotic fountains.

But if I could do none of this,
I hope you'll understand
That things are not what matters.
I love you as my man.

It's Your Birthday. Celebrate!

I'm sorry I did not get you
A birthday card or gift.
It feels like the middle of my brain
Is just a giant rift.

I know that there's gray matter there,
But it's so hard to find.
Our old dog died; my heart seems cracked.
I feel like I've lost my mind.

However, I want you to know
Your birthday's special too.
Although we lost a "special boy,"
I'm still in love with you.

We need to celebrate your life.
You're an amazing man.
I'm grateful God made me your wife.
He'll give us joy. He can.

To My Valentine

I tried to think what I could say,
Or else what I could do,
To let you know without a doubt
How much that I love you.

Some people like expensive gifts;
Others like receiving flowers.
But riches need not cost big bucks,
Nor fade in days or hours.

Others like me like our chocolate,
With caramel or nuts,
But sadly all that sugar
Is not good for our guts.

I might try to make you something
That's special just for you,
But our ever-changing weather's
Made that very hard to do.

I could clean our kitchen or garage,
But those don't stay clean long.
A massage would help your feet or back
If my hands were nice and strong.

Romantic poems might thrill my beau,
But they're not my expertise.
I'd rather spend my time with you
Doing whatever we please.

When I spend some daily time with Him
And let Him lead my life,
I have much more of His Love to give
And can be a better wife.

My daily actions and my words
Should His Love always show.
A tender touch, adoring glance
Let my beloved know

That love's not just a feeling,
A fickle, changing mood,
Or even just a mind made up
To always do what's good.

As people we're not able,
No matter how we try,
So I'll put my efforts in His hands,
And I'll run, or soar, or fly.

He said to run the race, not quit,
Or wait on Him and soar
Like eagles flying in the sky
As we trust him more and more.

So I put our marriage in His hands,
My beloved, our children too,
And I hope that you will always know
How much that I love you.

For My Valentine

I love how you nurture when I'm sad or down.
I love how you laugh when I'm joking around.
I love how you hug me when I need your hugs,
I love that we search with our grandkids for bugs.

I love that you let me drive your nice car,
And you fill it with gas when you know I'll go far.
I love that you cook so much better than me
And enjoy cooking more. How blessed could I be!

I love that you know God and call Him your Dad,
'Cause when He is in charge of our marriage, I'm glad.
And your prayers to your Father in Heaven delight,
But I'll stop and get ready to go out tonight.

A Valentine Wish

Roses are red, not green or blue.
I was smitten when I first met you.
They're also pink and white and yellow.
I'm so glad that you're my fellow.

Roses don't grow for everyone,
At least not me, with my brown thumb.
I love receiving them anyway.
Enjoy a Happy Valentine's Day!

A Father's Day Poem

Father's Day is finally here.
It's time for cheese dip, chips, and beer;
But wait! Grandkids will soon arrive.
Let's finish food and look alive.

There's pork and chicken, coleslaw too,
And potato salad just for you.
We're crowded in, but don't you fear,
'Cause a great-grandbaby will be here.

She'll meet her cousins who'll adore
The pretty baby, but not more
Than Papa does and Nana too.
We look forward to seeing all of you.

I hope you enjoy your special day,
We'll eat and talk; the kids will play.
You're a fun-loving Papa, a caring dad,
And the most loving husband I've ever had.

Happy Father's Day!

Twenty Years

Twenty years is quite a feat
For two who fell in love,
With heavy baggage in their hands
And a nudge from God above.

He watched them snip some loose ends
And tear at outer shells
They'd spent so long in building,
Trying to protect themselves.

But God knew walls between them
Would keep them far apart.
He wanted to do surgery
On hurts hiding in their hearts.

Like two great cats in a metal cage
They swung their powerful paws,
Ripping at the wound-scarred hearts
With hurtful words, like claws.

It wasn't God's best plan for them,
But their marriage should still work.
Their pride and stubbornness were strong;
It was time to heal, though hurt.

They acted out, gave their best shots
To keep their spouse away
From walled-in hurts they'd stuffed inside
In earlier anguished days.

But God desired to help them,
Not leave them hurting there:
They should cast off pride, repent, forgive.
They realized this during prayer.

With counseling they learned techniques
For the "other one" to use.
"If I give up my rights, give in,
He might win; I might lose."

He wanted her to end it,
So he wouldn't be surprised.
His demands to end their marriage
Brought pain, tears to her eyes.

He thought arguing meant it's over,
Not attempts to be understood.
When he argued as a boy,
That meant he wasn't good.

If she wasn't happy with their life,
Why stay and feel more pain?
He didn't believe she'd heard God say,
"Beloved, he's the man."

God said He'd chosen him for her:
He's handsome, and he's strong.
His heart's for God, like David's,
Even when he does things wrong.

They both have faults and deep hurts,
But with God's help they could heal
And shine for Him like diamonds,
So men would know He's real.

They should be patient with each other
And committed to their love.
God's always by their sides, it's true.
He's not just up above.

He'll comfort them when needed,
Give strength to them and peace.
They must trust God, believe His words,
And not let their union cease.

Though sometimes they lived far apart,
Their love remained, was true.
God helped them learn to love His way.
He'll do the same for you.

A Blessing for Our Daughter on Her Wedding Day

As you start your new journey as husband and wife,
Make sure that you welcome the Lord in your life.
He's the One who can tell you what you need to do.
When you're down, He brings joy as He says, "I love you."

Your new spouse is forever the love of your life,
But you're human, so occasionally there might be some strife.
Think of Jesus' example even when friends denied,
He forgave, showed them love, wanted them by His side,

For He knew that He'd soon face His trials in the world.
With your love at your side it's not nearly as hard.
Stand as one when you face what will come in your lives:
Mountain tops, a few valleys, the vast stars in the skies.

God has said that He knows His great plans for your lives,
He brings hope to your future as you prosper and thrive.
He does not wish you harm; He's not that kind of Dad.
He loves you so much, He gave the first Son He had.

He calls you His children, wants what's best for you,
Can you be like His Son, as He makes one from two?
He now blesses the union of your lives into one.
As you walk into the sunset, keep your eyes on the Son.

"For I know the plans that I have for you,"
declares the Lord, "plans for prosperity and not for disaster,
to give you a future and a hope."
(Jeremiah 29:11 NASB):

Darts

Sarcasm oozed from his taut lips,
Clouded the gleam in his eye.
He could have simply helped her then
Or even asked her, "Why?"

Instead he chose a poisonous dart
And aimed at her with flare.
He knew her weak spots, how to shoot.
He left her bleeding there.

The task at hand was simple,
Not really a big deal,
But when avoided in this way,
The poison starts to kill.

It doesn't hurt the body,
But pierces to the soul.
The things that die are trust and love.
Their "oneness" has a hole.

He shot the words out, then forgot.
He says he didn't do it,
At least not how she says he did.
She'll *always* overdo it.

The incident is not discussed.
He says it didn't happen.
She ought to keep it in her head
And stop her lips from flappin'.

That little hole begins to tear
Until it's deep and wide.
The many hurts not dealt with then
No longer can they hide.

The Lord tells us to deal with hurts,
With love, as they occur.
If not, they fester deep inside,
Become a giant blur.

It's hard to know the truth by now.
It's easier to blame.
Who's right; who's wrong? What details?
They start to play the game.

What started this huge cavern
That's tearing them apart?
The little things, no longer small,
Explode a hurting heart.

She asked him to fix something.
He said, "Get off my back.
I know I need to do it,
But won't when I get flack."

He wanted a clean kitchen,
So left her little hints,
Like "Don't you care if it's a mess?"
She glared and ate her mints.

They could just help each other,
Do things they know they should,
But that won't ever happen
Until the *other* one is "good."

They move along in silence,
Pretending they don't see,
The other person in the room.
They read or watch TV.

How could they fix the pattern
They've set up in their life?
Could they seek help, admit their wrongs,
Or muddle through the strife?

The Lord commands forgiveness,
If they repent or not.
It's for our peace he tells us,
With His blood it's been bought.

She's starting to feel better.
The pain is fading some.
The Word has helped her outlook,
The Spirit took her glum.

She smiles at her dear husband,
And rubs his neck and head.
"OK. Now no more stalling.
Come help me make the bed!"

(No matter how small the incident that
starts a fight, sometimes a couple needs
to take a step back. If one person can let
go of their anger, improved communication
and reconciliation will often follow.)

Judging Beauty, Judging People

The beholder can see
If it's beautiful or not.
It it's ugly, he knows it,
With the talent he's got.

She says labeling art
Is what art critics do,
But labels aren't meant
For me or for you.

God created us all
In His image, He says.
Should we judge if His handiwork
Fits our ideas?

She won't meet his ideal
Of a true, loving wife.
If not focused on him,
It's her fault there is strife.

To ignore, not submit,
Is an odious slight.
How can she be so wrong,
When he is so right?

Does she first look to God,
Then to him, last to others
To determine her actions,
How to be a good mother?

She says that God told her
His plans for her life,
But if God didn't tell *him*,
Why would God tell his wife?

Could it be that *she* listens
For God's quiet voice?
Instead of his yelling,
He could make this his choice.

She's heard all his tirades
About her mistakes.
Then he blames her children—
That their marriage could break.

She says she would like
For the marriage to last,
But they must confront
Stumbling blocks from their pasts.

If they look to the Lord
And make changes they should,
God would still mend their union,
As only He could.

God's made beauty from ashes
In the past, why not now?
If we're humble, receptive,
He will still show us how.

Can I Give It to Him?

My heart aches; my head feels like it might explode.
I can't keep on carrying this burdensome load.
Why is the responsibility mine?
I'm a wife, mom, and daughter; I should make it all fine.

And although I do know that assumption's not true,
It's not any easier when there's so much to do.
As a "doer," I feel I must do it myself;
As a mom, I reach out when my kids call for help.

My parents are aging; housework's hard to maintain.
My dad can't remember, just can't wake up his brain.
While my mom's getting tired, can't do what she'd like,
Her demanding behavior makes her seem like a tyke.

As I try to determine what relief they might need,
My doctor and friend give advice I don't heed:
"You're not always the answer to everyone's woes."
Still, in circles I run and trip o'er my own toes.

I know I must learn that it isn't my job
To be all things to all who approach with a sob.
"Can you help with my child?" "Can you help me clean house?"
Mom says, "I need help NOW!" I feel like a louse.

I was hoping to work on my writing today,
Or perhaps paint a picture, make jewelry, just play.
Maybe reading a book would be so much fun
That I might just ignore all the things that aren't done.

Can legitimate claims on my time not be right
As I help short-term needs some days or some nights?
I should consider my health and my husband's desires.
Does he have my time, too, as I put out their fires?

I now must admit that I'm just not the one
Who should take all their problems; it's God's only Son
Who can bear all our burdens, dry tears, heal disease.
Then we're free to enjoy God's joy and His peace.

Our Nights before Christmas

'Twas the week before Christmas,
And all through our house
Two old people were stirring.
There better not be a mouse!

She was going through papers
And lost track of the time.
He woke up, went to pee,
And had to see if she's fine.

He stayed up for a while,
Till she was ready for bed.
Allergies and congestion
Stopped up both of their heads.

Cedar pollen was everywhere,
On both cars and the ground.
Feral cats from three litters
In their backyard abound.

She's been drawing some pictures
For her sister's new book.
You do not need to ask her;
She'll request that you look.

Her computer is loaded
With family photos galore.
She's wondering if it discovered
How to duplicate more.

She has drawers of old documents
On too many shelves.
When Christmas is over,
Could she hire Santa's elves?

A young friend scans old letters,
Knows our family's names,
Likes how they stayed connected—
Wishes hers did the same.

43

Some of Momma's museum
Is now in our home.
Family history's so real,
Seeing purses and combs.

Metal teacups are chipped,
But Mom probably had fun
Having tea with her dollies
Or maybe some friends.

With Pa watching TV
And Ma doing crafts,
They take a break with some eggnog
And look for some snacks.

In September Covid got us,
Then attacked us where we're weak.
His blood pressure went up too high.
She just wanted to breathe.

Someone else did Thanksgiving.
We got to visit, not clean.
The food was delicious.
There was so much to eat.

Mid-December she honored
A year since her mom's death.
They toasted 31 years
Of a marriage God blessed.

As Christmas gets closer,
We have no gifts to give,
But our time and our love
And being thankful to live.

We have such a large family
Who still love each other, too.
May God bless you and love you,
As He loves to do.

Merry Christmas!

—— 4 ——

Parents

What Is a Dad?

A dad is a person who knows how to fix
Almost anything that you can break.
A dad is a person who's willing to give
A lot more than he ever takes.

A dad is a person who's willing to love you,
No matter what you might do.
A dad is a person who doesn't condemn;
He forgives and lets you be "you."

A dad likes to hold and play with your children
Whenever he gets the chance.
He'll show them how to play a game
Or watch them sing and dance.

He may be a man of but a few words,
So you listen whenever you can.
A dad you love, admire, respect.
He's a special kind of man.

Dad on stilts he made,
showing grandkids
how to use them.

Father

Dad fixing VW Bug

To someone who gives us all that he can—
The World's Greatest Father,
The World's Greatest Man.
To someone who gives, yet rarely gets in return,
Who loves and protects and always shows true concern.
To someone who helps his children and wife
So much that it almost becomes his whole life,
Who fixes this car and that toy and those old machines.
When it comes to frustration, he knows what it means.
To the man who has patience that's almost unreal,
Who knows how to love, who knows how to feel.
To the World's Best Father and Husband, it's true,
We want you to know that we all love you, too.

Dads and Daughters

I find it amusing that a man cannot stand
The rantings and ravings of another man,
Who puts down his daughter, the second man's wife,
But ignores how he's acted for most of his life.

His harsh words could pierce a girl's soul, break her heart;
And all of his fury could have torn her apart.
"She ignores me, forgets me; her motives are bad!"
Does he not remember she, too, has a dad?

Different Points of View

The young boy was hyper
As he bounced all around.
First he's here; then he's there.
Next he's up and he's down.

The man gets frustrated
As the child moves around.
"Why can't he be still,
Not squirm, make no sound?"

The man pushes buttons,
Moves the screen up and down.
He must figure it out;
The instructions aren't found.

The time doesn't matter.
It's the learning that counts,
Though the movie has started,
Through the lists he has bounced.

How can he be flustered
At what the boy likes to do,
When his similar actions
Aggravate others too?

The Inspiring, Inimitable, Knowledgeable, Noble Nonagenarian

(For Dad's 90th Birthday)

It's hard to believe you have finally arrived
At an age that few men reach.
You have been a role model all of your life;
By your actions you would teach.

We learned to be honest, helpful, and kind
To someone who had needs.
The neighborhood kids and men at the church
Valued your knowledge and deeds.

Though you didn't speak much, when you finally did,
We knew that we should hear.
The well-thought words you would impart
Could make us laugh to tears.

They could also maybe make us think
Like we never had before,
But sometimes if we'd misbehaved
We knew our behinds would be sore.

Though ninety years have slowed you down
A little in some ways,
I'm thankful that you've been my dad
And blessed me all my days.

To Mom for Mother's Day

Mother's Day has come and gone,
And I got you no card.
I thought of it, but never did,
'Cause I was working hard.

I painted shelves for one child
On Thursday until eight.
I painted in my office
On Friday till too late.

On Saturday we painted
From noon until near ten.
Now someone's master bed and bath
Look awesome once again.

He's trying to sell his own big house
To move in with my kids,
So pray they get the house they want
And his house gets good bids.

On Sunday I moved furniture
To paint more office walls.
I remixed paint and finished two;
I couldn't do them all.

On Monday I took Daddy
For a shot in his right eye.
They dilate both for pictures;
It's hard to see outside.

We parked at your house near the curb.
Dad stepped into the yard.
As I moved toward your front door,
He fell down really hard.

I turned to see what happened.
He fell back and hit his head.
He lay there dazed for seconds,
Tried to sit. "Stay still," I said.

I needed to get help for him,
But didn't want to go
For fear he'd try to stand again.
I had to tell him, "No!"

I yelled for you; you didn't hear.
The neighbor heard and came.
She watched Dad till I could get help.
His balance ain't the same.

His recovery last summer
When he was very ill
Amazed his wife and children,
As he walks or shuffles still.

On Tuesday with my daughter,
We painted shelves until it rained.
Then we picked up our granddaughter,
Brought her here, and still stayed sane.

On Wednesday I stayed home to rest,
My legs and feet in pain.
My husband moved a desk to help.
I painted once again.

I finished one wall, moved more stuff,
And did the final wall.
I moved stuff back and put things up.
I was so tired I could fall.

On Thursday and on Friday
I did fun things, useful too:
Painted frames to match the pictures
And scrapbooked old cartoons.

So now you know why there's no card,
But a long list of excuses.
Besides, I know you give your cards
To our kids for their re-uses.

The Legacy

At first it was faith, family, and fun
That fashioned the fabric from which she had come.
Then later in life with a large legacy,
From grandmas and grandpas and those in between,
She made a museum, a music room too.
With all the sheet music, now what will she do?

There are Bibles and books and baubles galore,
Vintage clothes in the armoire, vintage shoes on its floor.
A Civil War overcoat, bayonet, shot,
And the Bible and Atlas Grandpa never forgot
Are some of the items displayed as real treasures.
Grandma made hats; we still have her feathers.

Antique china predating the Civil War
Is near cobbler's leather in a box on the floor.
Grandpa's cobbler tools and some boots that he made,
Near the crimpers she used to fix curls on her head,
An old porcelain doll, a white china pitcher,
Near the medical herbs—are just part of the picture.

As we open more boxes of papers and books,
We sort into medical, army, and such.
Then we find clothing, linens, and lace.
The moldy material gets too close to my face.
We wash it, and fold it, and stack it until
It looks less like old linens and more like a hill.

The museum and music room are mostly done,
Letters, pictures, and ironing now crowd the front room.
The photos are hidden in their closet space,
But recycling papers are all over the place.
We're still in transition for over a year;
Could that be why others don't rush over here?

Now closets, clothes, sewing, Mom's shrinking, and more
Account for the stacks all over her floors.
Her sewing room's full, and more stuff is upstairs.
Her various stacks are draped over the chairs.
Clothes today are not quality like they once were,
So we keep what we have, like they all did before.

Her interests have changed to family and church,
Getting to Heaven if she's just good enough,
Reading from her new Bible, with all of its notes,
Then sitting with Dad and watching her shows.
But her favorite thing now everyone knows—
Redoing her closet and all of her clothes.

The heirs who inherit this heiress's hoard
Will have plenty to do, should not soon get bored.
The letters tell much about past family—
Whether sharp tongued, fascinating, or funny, as can be.
The photos amuse, show which DNA's strong.
Faith and love were the answer, even when we were wrong.

Our family's not perfect; we've made our mistakes,
But I'd trade for no others; I accept what He makes.
Our family's legacy of faith, love, and fun
Are displayed in their letters over and over again.
They accepted His gifts of mercy and love.
I look forward to seeing them someday above.

The Right Hairstyle

The white-haired lady
Looks in the mirror
And thinks of times now past.
She sees the lines
And wonders why
Her beauty cannot last.

She gets a perm.
She told them how
To roll it to look right.
At home she cries,
"They did it wrong!"
She can't go out that night.

She can't explain
To anyone
Just how her hair should look,
But gets upset
If they suggest
She find a style in a book.

She finally tells
The one doing her hair
That she wanted a look from the 30s.
Why'd she wait to explain
The desired look at the end,
So the stylist and she were now hurting?

Could it be that the look
So desired's in no book,
But comes from memories past?
When she looks in the mirror,
She sees wrinkles and frizz,
Wonders why youthful beauty can't last.

She covers her perm
With the hat in her hand,
Before going into the stores.
When she finally gets home,
Her hair sticks out all weird;
She feels she is right to be sore.

Her daughter asks her
To describe the hairstyle
She envisions, if she can.
She wants soft, pretty curls
By the side of her face—
Not this frizz that's as short as a man's.

The girl shows her a photo
Of the mom at sixteen.
Is this the look she would like?
But the mom just can't tell,
As she stares at the teen,
Says, "The hair in the photo's not white."

Mom at 16 years old

Fixating on Figures or Faces?

Fixating on figures
Of family and friends
Is futile—they fluctuate,
Again and again.

Fixate on their faces—
The eyes to their soul
Or their smiles that bring warmth
And can make you feel whole.

Fixate on your Savior.
Love like He tells you to,
For the past slights of others
Can't hurt them; only you.

Hurts held tight make you bitter.
You lose sight of the good—
That others readily matured
And loved you as they should.

Do you reflect your Savior
To your kids and your friends,
Or dwell on others' past wrongs
Without making amends?

We know no one is perfect,
But God's plan we can trust.
As we help those in need,
It takes our eyes off of us.

When we model God's love,
It draws others to Him,
And we're much better company
For our friends and our kin.

As your memories fade,
Do you give up the past
Slights and errors of others
Or cling to them fast?

While you make final plans,
Knowing your time is near,
From all of your past,
What memories are dear?

Is his handsome face smiling
As he kisses your face?
Is he always beside you,
Traveling with you each place?

Was he forever faithful,
Though his memory was poor?
Do you see his face light up
As you walk through the door?

What manner of memories
Should we now have of you?
Did you radiate God's love,
Show your children God's truth?

What Happened to My Mom?

My real mom is hiding inside of the skin
Of the woman who sits in her chair with a pen,
Circling words in a book, or perhaps asking me
To help find the words that, so far, she can't see.

My mom liked to dress up in her beautiful clothes,
Added jewelry and makeup, looked good head to toe.
With a few closets full of nice clothes she had sewn
And some bought; quite the fashion collection she owned.

But *this* woman for days wears the same top and pants.
She acts like Mom sometimes, shows off with a dance.
She likes to tell jokes, so I think Mom is home,
But then she has vanished just as fast as she'd come.

It's hard not to love her; to me she gave birth;
But her changing behavior makes me oft' doubt my worth
To the woman who now likes to boss me around,
As I help her and take her to doctors in town.

We knew for a while that Mom had OCD.
It must be done her way—dot I's and cross T's.
At 90, Mom was tested; she has ADHD.
Now her half-finished projects make more sense to me.

She used to bark orders for what I should do.
"Don't touch that." "Pick this up." "Take all this with you."
I explained that my house size is about half of hers,
But my protests just fell on a pair of deaf ears.

My mom had six boys; that would drive others mad.
She became a "drill sergeant," sometimes even to Dad.
Her attempts to control our behavior was seen
As "teaching us discipline," or "Man, she is mean!"

I wouldn't have wanted near that many kids,
But the decision is not fully ours; it is His.
Having nine would have driven me over the edge,
But Mom loved us all as she danced on the ledge.

Now she wonders why most her kids don't come to visit.
Could it be that she speaks, but won't bother to listen?
Besides some being far, they don't come 'cause they fear
Being talked to like children, or ignored, while they're here.

I don't like dementia—what it does to her brain:
Not just altering her mind, but causing anguish and pain
To the one in its clutches and to her child who tries
To help Mom, who's declining, till I can't help but cry.

It destroys her memories, from her present and past,
And slows down her movements, so she can't do things fast.
It made Daddy shuffle when he tried to walk,
Mom falls asleep easily as someone else talks.

I want to give up and quit: "I can't help anymore,"
I occasionally think as I leave her front door.
Then I think of the fun mom that she often could be.
What will my kids do if this happens to me?

Maturing versus Aging

The woman has talents that still go unused.
When you're trying to tell her, she just starts to snooze.
Like most all of us, she's beginning to find
That aging quite often can be most unkind.

She once liked to sew, tole paint, and quilt,
But her shoulder cartilage started to wilt.
It withered away and brought her such pain.
She attempted to use her skills, but in vain.

She now believes her purpose in life
Is to make folks laugh to forget all their strife.
Many tell her that she has just made their day,
For laughter can heal, can be fun like play.

She reads some new jokes, and retells some old.
Her kids simply wish that she were not so bold.
She approaches new people almost anywhere.
Many like the distraction, but some will just stare,

For they don't understand a word that she says.
They're embarrassed to tell her it's over their heads.
She says she can pick out the ones who will laugh,
But when they don't speak English, it can be quite a gaffe.

The woman won't let this mistake slow her down,
Like getting back up when one falls to the ground.
If it embarrasses her kids, that makes it more fun;
'Cause they did it to her till she wished they were done.

I also have seen that old age can be cruel:
I signed up for ballet and felt like a fool.
Metal hips had restrained how my body could bend;
Dorsal bunions made twirling come to a quick end.

Low impact aerobics may be now what I need.
Fantasia hippos seemed more like my speed.
Ballet might belong to the things in my past,
But I'll still like to *dance* for as long as I last.

Maybe Solomon was right about seasons in life.
Not maturing with grace can make dissonance rife.
If we fear that our children are trying to remove
Our choices, we don't see when their motive is love.

To attempt to maintain what we think we have lost,
We may treat them as children, spew demands, try to boss,
But talking to adult children like they're kids causes pain,
Makes them angry, not wanting to help you again.

Thankfully, they learned love when Mom gave them her all.
This helped them to return, in spite of the gall.
If a person lets bitterness into her life
For slights real or imagined, it eventually brings strife.

If someone's rudeness offended so she cannot let go,
Often reminding others of those hurts long ago,
It could have made her grow bitter, and maybe resent,
Not releasing her "right" to get even, repent.

Forgiving is more than just words; it's an act
Of letting go of the hurt and desire to get back
At the ones who have hurt us, or maybe their kin.
Staying mad at dead people is probably a sin.

Do I dislike the pain someone caused in the past?
Yes, but I must give it up; Christ says it can't last.
He's forgiven us all; that's what we need to do.
Do we think others' sins worse than what we may do?

Give the Savior your hurts, the bitterness too,
And resentments or anger; it's the best thing for you.
Love your parents, your children and those who've been mean.
You may be the only Jesus they've seen.

He's reflected in you, as you let Him be.
Let his strengths take your frailties, His love be what all see.
Aging needn't be awful, though it does slow us down,
He helps us mature, wisdom wear like a crown.

Christmas Time at My House

'Twas two weeks before Christmas,
When all through my house
Were old things from my mom's
To fix, share, or throw out.

There's a rocker Mom bought
When she moved to Bellaire,
To rock three baby brothers,
But it didn't end there.

I refinished, re-cushioned it,
'Ere my first child was born.
Then I did it again,
When that child had a son.

Years later I stained it,
Made new cushions for Mom.
She enjoyed it till she went
To a memory care home.

It's at my house again,
Rocked my new great-granddaughter.
Will it stay here or go?
It will be where it "ought'er."

Then there's Great-Uncle Bruce's
Army trunk from the war
Back in the 1940s—
Now I have it "restored."

The top had a hole
Too large to repair.
Now it's lined and repainted
For clothes little girls wear.

There's a dowel rod to hang clothes
And a shelf for much more.
It now stands on its side
And has a newly-made door.

I remade my dance costumes
That my mom made for me,
Made skirts to go with them
And accessories.

I used great-grandmas' sheer curtains
To make fancy white skirts,
Lined a lingerie top—
Cut it down—now it works.

I used material I had
To make more skirts and tops.
Dress-up clothes were my focus:
A full trunk made me stop.

An apothecary cabinet
Once belonging to Bruce
Holds military and medical
Important papers and loot.

Behind the couch are mementos
Of Grandpa Israel Mack,
Who fought in the Civil War
About 150 years back.

Some tools and old leather
He used to make boots and shoes
Are displayed to remind us
That the path that we choose

Affects those all around us,
And others, as well.
His dad and granddad were preachers.
Grandpa's faith you could tell.

We have letters he wrote
To Corinia, his wife.
He reminded her of his love,
How God was real in their lives.

I framed some unique feathers
Grandma used to make hats.
Brilliant seamstress and milliner,
She left clothes to prove that.

The National Civil War Museum
In Harrisburg will some day
Show the Macks' photos, papers,
And treasures in a display.

Books and music were valued
By our ancestors too:
Hymnals, Bibles, and history.
They wrote poetry too.

Our family loved learning.
Had books for languages galore.
Some could speak French & German.
From books and trips they learned more.

Grandma Mack, although sixty,
Learned German as well.
Their newspapers, antiques,
Quite the story they tell—

Lindbergh flew to many places;
McKinley died while President;
Germans bombed so much of Europe;
Coronations were big events.

Though the living room's cluttered,
My office is a maze.
I avoid obstacles or hurdles,
With frequent changes, many ways.

I am going through my papers,
Though it's taking way too long.
I'm planning soon to share with others
What I can't handle alone.

My family's history's important,
But what details do we need?
Digitizing papers and photos
May be digitizing me.

I want to clean up this clutter,
I repurpose what I can,
Share the wealth with those who want it—
It's in my blood; that's who I am.

I'm finding things that I'd forgotten,
Or finding time to do tasks,
With priority levels ever changing,
Before Christmas has passed.

Our family saved their many treasures,
And now I'm sharing them with you.
May their love for God and family
Give you a Merry Christmas, too.

6

Children and Grandchildren

Thirteen!

(for my first daughter)

You are thirteen! You have passed through the threshold and entered
that seemingly magical world of the teenager.

You are no longer "just an adolescent" with a body and emotions that
are changing; you have "arrived."

Your desire for freedom has increased at a sometimes alarming rate.

You are ready for a test of wills: yours versus mine or "ours" (meaning anyone in authority).

You feel safe within limits or boundaries, but you like to see how
elastic you can make them with your pleading or pouting.

Unfortunately, when a rubber band or any elastic stretches too far,
it usually pops and someone gets hurt.

Changing, testing, crying, pouting, laughing; all of these are part
of being a teenager.

You want to move from childhood to adulthood at your pace, but
your pace keeps changing, and sometimes even goes backwards.

You want all of the privileges of an adult, but few or none of the responsibilities that go
along with them.

You like to promote your own ideas, not those of your parents,
provided, of course, they are accepted by your friends.

A teenager is somewhere between childhood and maturity,
moving toward the better judgment we hope to have as adults.

You have entered into an exciting new experience; enjoy it!

Who and what you are when you come out at the other end is
determined by you and all your choices.

Learn to be wise. Learn who to turn to for help. Learn to be you!

Thirteen!

(for my second daughter)

You have arrived, you think.

You have entered into that magical realm of the "teenager."

But what is a teenager?

According to the dictionary, it is merely "a person between the ages of thirteen and nineteen, inclusive, an adolescent."

However, when you are one, you know what it really is.

You have passed forever from being a "child" to being a "teen."

It is a state of mind, a mixture of emotions and hormones not previously experienced, as well as the all-too-noticeable physical changes.

It is being on the brink of becoming an adult, without realizing that many careless moves can lead to a drastic fall, while following that narrow and almost indiscernible path laid out by the Master Planner can take you step by step across a bridge to the other side.

Many call out from both sides, and even below, telling you how to make it, but listen closely to the "wee small voice" put within you as a young child, for it is the one that will tell you the precise steps laid out for you.

Although we're each tempted to try to look and act like everyone else, each of us is unique, with our own plan.

Parents are your guides from childhood to adulthood; they can often help you avoid pitfalls with which they are all too familiar, either from their own experiences or those of others they know.

If you listen carefully, you can often hear the wisdom disguised as orders, rules, complaints, or even suggestions.

It's time for you to test your independence, your ability to make decisions for yourself, for at the end of the road, as an adult, you will be making most all of them by yourself.

You will soon realize that with new privileges come new responsibilities. Learn how to make right choices, where to turn for the right kind of help.

Don't be afraid to ask questions; it's a sign of wisdom, not weakness.

Take it slowly; if you try to rush things, you'll miss a lot more. You'll get to the other side at the right place and the right time if you follow the Master's directions carefully and don't skip around.

Most of all, enjoy the trip.

God bless your new journey!

Happy Belated Birthday, Daughter

I didn't get one at the store.
I'd get the food and think, "There's more."
I'd get back home and think real hard,
Remember I'd forgot the card.
This silly mother is forlorn
For not remembering her firstborn!

Her entrance to the world was wild—
My Super Bowl Sunday beautiful child.
Her dad, anxious to see the game,
Loved her speed, when out she came.
She hasn't slowed down much since then.
She's smarter than most groups of men:

Worked hard in school, at work, at home
Until at last she's finally come
To be "the boss," be recognized
For titles and degrees so prized.
Though I am proud of these things too,
Her inner beauty is what shines through.

She showed compassion as a child
To a girl being bullied; instead she smiled
And took her to a counselor who could help.
She could care for others as well as herself.
Self-reliant then, as she is today,
She keeps busy—not much stands in her way.

I hope that your birthday was a wonderful one,
Nice and relaxing with husband and son.
I hope that you know that I love you so much,
Even when I can be so out of touch
With what is important—not boxes and papers—
But being with family in fun and wild capers.

Although this poem sounds pretty funny,
I didn't not get the card for the money.
I simply forgot when I should have been thinking
And only remembered when the TV was blinking
And telling of playoffs and the Super Bowl game,
And that's my excuse no matter how lame.

Our Grandson

....

(At Eleven Years Old)

Our grandson isn't perfect.
He may gripe and may complain,
And even get real grumpy,
Till I ask him to refrain.

Our grandson, usually happy,
May sometimes pout and whine,
But I'd trade him for no other.
I'm proud that he is mine.

Our grandson is quite handsome.
He's smart and funny, too.
Making friends for him is simple,
'Cause he knows the Golden Rule.

He wishes kids would act right,
And he wants them to be fair:
He thinks they're being immature
And wonders if they care.

In math he's quite a genius.
He began computer games
And could play to many levels,
Before he could read the names.

Our grandson isn't perfect,
But he's as close as he can be.
His parents and his Savior
Keep him sweet for you and me.

Katie

We love little Katie.
Her smile is so sweet.
She sucks on her fingers
And nibbles her feet.

She laughs, and she giggles
And "talks" to us all.
It's amazing how smart
She can be, when so small.

She's pretty and precious
To all of her kin.
One smile from sweet Katie,
And your heart she will win.

Our Grandson at Fourteen

From the time he was born,
He brought all of us joy.
He cuddled and grinned—
Our cute baby boy.

He began to sit up
And soon started to crawl,
Then pulled himself up,
Till he stood there so tall.

He took a few steps;
Suddenly he could run.
He sometimes fell down,
But exploring was fun.

He soon learned to climb
On whatever he could—
The doctor's wire toys
Or a half-wall of wood.

He understood numbers
And learned wrong from right,
But once hid with a doughnut—
Gave his mom such a fright.

He roughhoused with Daddy
And watched him play games.
He could do the maneuvers,
Knew the characters' names.

Then his dad let him play
Without all the gore,
But he needed help reading
The instructions for war.

He learned numerals quickly,
Then letters and sounds.
Soon words made it easy
To move players around.

His mom usually took him
Wherever she'd go,
Whether visiting or shopping;
She thought he should know

How important and special
He was to her then
And forever would be,
Whether baby or man.

She would read to him often,
Play with him and his toys,
Let him help her make cookies,
Watch him run and make noise.

At school he excelled,
And good friends he made.
He joined soccer and scouts,
And piano he played.

He learned music quickly,
Memorizing each song—
Played from memory at a concert,
In just seven weeks long.

They moved closer to Nana,
Started over again.
With a new school and new friends.
Would the changes not end?

He joined band and played trumpet,
Learned the music quite fast,
Stayed in scouts, learned robotics,
Which he thinks is a blast.

Now he's taller than Mom,
Isn't done growing yet,
But his smile's what you notice
And his eyes, I would bet.

A caring young man—
You can see it in his eyes.
He is helpful and kind;
For a teen he is wise.

He loves his little sister;
She adores "Bubby" so.
He gives hugs and is thankful—
The best young man I know.

Our Princess

She likes to wiggle,
And she likes to giggle,
And she likes to snuggle up.

She kicks her toys,
And she smiles at boys,
And she likes to watch my pup.

She's a little cutie
And a sweet patootie,
And she loves to grin and yack.

She cries for her bottle,
Caused her mom to waddle,
But we wouldn't give her back.

She's her Papa's princess.
When she screams, he winces.
She's a pretty little doll.

She likes to blow bubbles.
Mom's work time has doubled.
She's the greatest gift of all.

How I love to watch her.
She looks like my daughter
When she was a little girl.

She has precious clothes on,
Lots of matching bows on
Where someday she'll have her curls.

She takes Mommy shopping,
Keeps her Daddy hopping
And her brother vigilant,

But they love to hold her
Snuggled to their shoulders,
For they know she's Heaven-sent.

Our Princess is sleeping,
And my puppy's creeping
To get back up in my lap.

Guess it's time to end now,
Have some clothes to mend now,
So I guess this is a wrap.

Twelve on the Twelfth and Tenaciously Testing as a Teen Prematurely

You just became twelve,
But you're fast on your way
To becoming a teen,
Anticipating the day.

So, what is a *teen*?
Can you explain the term?
It's an attitude, mindset,
New view of the world.

When you enter that realm,
You're no longer a *child*.
Your emotions and hormones
Can make you act wild.

You'll enter the path
To become an adult.
Some never quite get there,
Say it can't be their fault.

You, however, are blessed
To have parents who care,
Who know God's expectations
For getting you there.

Now "mature," you want privileges
To promote your prestige,
But Responsibility's link
To this rank you don't see.

Why can't you do this,
Get your way, or have that?
That won't make you grown-up;
It just makes you a brat!

Opportunities come
When you work hard like your dad.
Use the skills that God gave you;
You'll feel joyful, not sad.

You will ask lots of questions
To define who you are.
You'll pick truths you agree with,
But you don't need to go far.

Your parents have taught you
What they've learned through the years.
If you listen, obey them,
You will have fewer tears.

They've learned Wisdom's from God,
Not from fair-weather friends,
Who may stretch all their limits,
Till it pops their back ends.

As you know from experience,
Rubber bands can be fun,
Till they pop you or others;
Then you hurt or you run.

Now, what have you learned
From your parents so far?
Have they taught you how precious
To Jesus you are?

Do you know your true value,
As you're becoming a man?
God, your Daddy and Father,
Has laid out your plan.

As you spend time with your dad
And your mom, you have learned
What they like, how they love you,
How to have fun, take turns.

As you start to go out
With your friends, as you grow,
Will you make good decisions
And know when to say, "No!"?

If you need to ask someone
What they think you should do,
Ask your Father; he listens,
And He'll answer you too.

He won't yell or be loud,
So you must know His voice.
Get close to Him; He whispers,
But He'll be your best choice.

My Talented Grandson

My grandson is quite talented.
He is amusing too.
He likes to say what's on his mind,
Which may annoy you.

He doesn't really mean to.
His brain's wired differently.
God crafted him the way He wants,
With a plan for who he'll be.

It's hard for him to sit still.
His body tends to wiggle.
His efforts to control himself
Might even make you giggle.

If you will make the effort
To look past his twists and turns,
You may discover for yourself
There's a lot from him to learn.

When we built a treehouse with his help,
He almost talked non-stop,
For creative ideas flowed so fast,
If he didn't speak, he'd pop.

How his imagination worked that quickly
Was scarcely understood,
But his suggestions were so cool,
I would use all that I could.

As designer for a project
His innovative juices flowed.
His group created his designs;
For his class they made some dough.

We wish he would control himself,
But forget he's just a teen.
He has improved, but's not there yet.
His potential is still to be seen.

As adults, we want children quiet and still,
But express our emotions with might.
If emotions and impulses we can't control,
Why do we think they'll do it right?

Now I'm not condoning misbehavior in kids.
For that, consequences are due;
But how can we expect perfection in kids,
When it's something we can't even do?

Our grandson must continue to work on control
Of his movements and mouth all his life,
As we also accomplish this crucial goal,
We will learn it reduces our strife.

As this teen matures and gains wisdom,
His talents and gifts will amaze.
He can easily become an exceptional young man,
If he follows His plans all his days.

Terri

When Terri was a little girl,
Her grandpa would tell all,
"Her clear, fair skin and bright blue eyes
Look like a porcelain doll."

Her smile could take your breath away.
Her pouts could make you giggle.
She climbed on and in most anything.
Escaping, she might wiggle.

When she was close to four years old,
Her grandpa came to see her.
Her mom said she must go to bed;
She said, almost in tears,

"You're breaking my heart!"
How could we keep her from her favorite grandpa?
He brought a friend; her visit ends,
On order from her mom.

We couldn't keep a straight face then.
Her reasoning emotions
Caught us off guard and made us laugh—
A young girl with such notions!

The next day she had lots of time
To spend with everyone.
They talked and played and talked some more.
The love they shared was fun.

Patti

Sweet, pretty Patti
Once helped run the house.
She could talk up a blue streak
Or be quiet as a mouse.

If you couldn't find something,
She would know where to find
Your keys or most anything.
She's one of a kind.

She'd bring order from chaos;
Her mind could conceive
Where things were, what they'd need
When they'd pack up to leave.

She can play the piano,
Started learning the drums.
She's led children in singing,
And she probably hums.

She turned 18 last fall,
Has matured past her years;
Went through conflict that hurt,
But she learned through the tears.

Sometimes people we meet
Will not tell us the truth.
He may look like a sheep,
But inside is a wolf.

Since she's now a young lady
Thinking of a good mate,
She should ask God for wisdom,
Be content as she waits.

Integrity, honesty
Are what she should seek.
Although handsome and strong,
He should also be meek.

When I first met her grandpa,
The Lord said, "He's the one."
He didn't say it'd be easy,
But we both looked to Him.

We sometimes were apart;
We could then hear his voice.
When He gave us His peace,
We could make the right choice.

He's our Counselor, Advisor
If we give him our ear.
If we take his advice,
We have nothing to fear.

He wants only the best
For each child that He made.
With Him guiding our hearts,
Wisdom filling our heads,

Patti's future is bright
When wise choices she makes.
Repenting, being forgiven,
When she makes a mistake.

Her Mom and her siblings
Can also advise.
Hearing their words and God's;
Can really open her eyes.

The Lord knows her heart
Much better than me.
Her beauty outside and in
Is what I can see.

Patti's smart, energetic,
With a longing to learn.
As she works, goes to school,
She'll see how to discern.

Can this person be trusted
To do what he says?
If he's ornery or mean,
How will you act those days?

Growing up is a process,
Doesn't happen real fast.
With a godly foundation,
Her sweet nature should last.

Outer beauty is fleeting,
But not for a while.
Her eyes have a twinkle,
And say much with her smile.

Sweet, pretty Patti
Has her family's support
As she passes from teen
To adorable adult.

My Grandson Is Eighteen!

I can't believe that you're now eighteen.
You can vote, go to war, do most anything.
I am glad, however, you're not like most others.
You care for people, still give hugs, and listen to Mother's
Occasional suggestions or warnings, and her good advice.
She gives you space, lets you decide what to do with your life.

I am proud of the sensible young man that you are.
You have friends with like minds, but have learned to ignore
The kids who tease, misbehave, and act immature.
Though they're extremely annoying, your intentions are sure.
Why waste your time and attention on brats such as these,
When you can work and play hard, move toward goals as you please.

You've come a long way from the toddler who'd growl,
The babe who'd run, not walk, and then fall down and howl.
You understood math before numerals you read.
Though you shouldn't, you kept score, when only four, in your head.
You crawled over your dog, climbed up on a half-wall.
To Mom and your Nana, you were the cutest of all.

You've come quite a distance from your precarious ways.
Now you shoot friends with paint, stick to your computer for days.
You care for a dog that isn't your own
And keep an eye on your sister whenever she's home.
Though she can be a pain, you've loved her from her birth.
God made you unique, a young man of great worth.

I love you. Happy Belated Birthday!

A Birthday Wish

I know the wrapping's not so great,
But please know that I tried.
I saw no gift bag big enough.
What counts is what's inside.

I bought material 'fore I knew
The plans you'd made for school.
I hope you like it anyway.
It's still a useful tool.

Being 19's not a breeze.
You're standing on the brink
Of all life has in store for you.
It's not always what you think.

I speak from my experience,
And that of others, too.
Your choices, good or bad, don't rule
The man inside of you.

They definitely affect your life;
You know that all too well.
Who you become is still your choice,
And only time will tell.

You have ingenious talents;
You were clever as a tot,
Devising schemes to get things done,
Whether Mom said, "Yes," or not.

I've admired your fierce compassion,
Sense of what is wrong or right,
Wish for fairness if not justice.
I believe your future's bright.

Happy Belated 19th Birthday!

Waiting for Wonky Weather

I'm glad that we're not driving in this noisy, flashing mess.
Your Daddy checked the weather; then he said that this was best.
He wants his Katie safe and sound, her Nana, Papa, too.
Can't wait until the morning, when we decide what we will do.

I've been cutting out and sewing way too many dress-up clothes.
I've made messes in the living room and office, as you know.
I couldn't do it otherwise; I just don't work that way.
I can't wait until my Katie gets here, so we can play.

I just realized again that you and I are so alike.
You have looked and acted like me since you were a little tyke.
I hope you've learned, as I have, that although we make a mess
When we're making and we're playing, cleaning up our mess is best.

Will see you soon!

Lacie

Lacie's turning 15.
She's growing up so fast.
We see her body's changes,
But her character's what lasts.

Her figure curves; her muscles strong
Help her excel at sports.
She feels cute in her swimsuit,
Shows off her legs in shorts.

But her heart is what God looks at,
As He assesses His design.
She loves His Son, her family,
Enjoys her elders most the time.

She loves the woman who once lived
Next door to their old home—
Went to see her on a recent trip,
Was glad that she had gone.

She went on a vacation
With her mom's dad and his wife.
They floated in the swimming pool
And relaxed from stress and strife.

They raced under the water
And did handstands till they fell.
They talked and laughed and talked some more.
Grandma scraped her chin. Oh, well.

Lacie's sis was there also;
An aunt with toddler too.
Then Mom and brother joined them.
That's what fun families do.

At fourteen and at fifteen,
Teens start to internalize
Their moral code to live by
From those who teach, and those who lie.

Her friends may tell her what they think,
How they should live their lives,
Or a stranger may expound on life,
Seen from his wayward eyes.

A good mom will teach her children
To make decisions on their own.
As they become self-motivated,
She knows part of her job is done.

Because Lacie naturally trusted,
Someone took advantage of her.
Now she speaks her mind, asserting her right
To protect herself and others from hurt.

Did her mama tell her *what* to think
Or actually teach her *how*?
One can lead to exploitation;
The other could allow

The child to determine where to turn
When her parents or teachers aren't there.
If she already talks to her Father,
She knows that He'll always hear.

It's not always easy for us to hear Him.
He's polite. He doesn't scream.
God whispers so you can hear His voice
When you're quiet and draw close to Him.

She likes to have fun with family and friends
Without spending lots of money,
Taking walks on the beach, watching sunsets at dusk,
Eating, shopping, and acting funny.

And so, dear Lacie, as you mature
Recall what God wants of you:
Do you listen to Him, use your gifts and your skills
To do what He wants you to do?

A Birthday Poem

You asked my daughter for her hand thirteen years ago.
Her complex personality you didn't truly know.
She didn't know you either, at least not like she thought,
But luckily for both of you, the Bible you were taught.

You learned of love—agape love—the way our God loves us.
You knew about commitment and learned in God to trust.
You have a handsome baby boy, as bouncy as they come.
Together now the three of you are creating your own home.

I want to tell you from the heart, I'm glad you joined our clan.
I think my daughter's choice was right, for you're a godly man.
Though neither of you know it all, you know where you can turn,
For our Savior and Creator offers all you need to learn.

I am glad that you are part of our family.

Welcome to Our Family

My daughter's team had worked with yours
For 15 years or so.
You stayed calm under pressure;
She asked questions like a pro.

Eventually, you asked her out.
She was pleasantly surprised.
When she told me she was dating you,
There was joy in her eyes.

You finally met her children.
Her son reacted like a teen—
Polite, respectful, "God for Mom."
He probably thought, "Let's wait and see."

Her toddler responded a different way.
She loved you from the start.
She called you "mine" when speaking your name.
You had easily won her heart.

As we watched you interacting
With our daughter and her kids,
We saw love, respect, compassion,
And we knew that you were His.

We're delighted that you have become
Part of our large family,
A godly friend for my husband,
A man revered by me.

You show your love for my daughter
In many different ways—
You love her children as your own,
Let her work on crafts for days.

You don't mind when she spends some time
With her sister or her mom—
If they shop for hours, lose track of time,
And she's late in getting home.

You also like to relax, hang out,
With your wife, her daughter and son,
Whether separately or together.
You use humor and have fun.

I guess what I am trying to say
Is that I hope your birthday's great,
That we're glad you married our daughter.
She has an excellent mate.

Your Lives

Don't live your lives so your kids must hear,
"Do as I say and not as I do."
But live so you can be proud of them,
And they can be proud of you.

(written many years ago, because I was tired of
hearing other adults recite this quote to children)

The Son

A beautiful boy adored his mom.
He thought she was his girlfriend.
His dad was gone; when he came back,
Her love came to an end.

He followed his dad wherever he'd go,
To fish or hunt or pray.
He'd imitate him all he could,
To be like him some day.

His dad was busy with three jobs;
He'd preach, teach school, and sell.
He loved his son with all his heart,
But didn't know him well.

His parents thought they did their part
To give him what he needed.
A loving touch, an "I love you"—
For this, his heart still pleaded.

Some teachers couldn't see beyond
The things he couldn't do.
They put him in a "know-nothing" class;
They didn't know the truth.

Yes, the boy learned differently,
Had trouble sitting still;
Focusing was difficult,
But their insults he could feel.

Sadly their words molded him,
Since no one stopped to say,
"He's just a little boy:
We can't treat him this way."

They didn't know how sensitive
A little child could be.
The careless words they uttered then
Might not hurt you or me.

He longed for their approval;
He wanted to belong.
The boy *was* intelligent—
The teachers' words were wrong!

How could the parents just not see
The pain brought on their son?
Could it have been the teachers weren't
The only careless ones?

Perhaps they could not understand
Things they had never learned.
They "stuffed" their pain, "got over it,"
But deep inside it burned.

Their goodness showed to all around.
He worked hard to provide.
She helped the neighbors, those in need.
The kids stayed by her side.

Her oldest was the model child.
She had the sweetest baby.
The middle two worked hard to win
Her love or notice, maybe.

She labeled *him* "rebellious son"
And called him the "black sheep."
He heard her tell a neighbor that,
When she thought he was asleep.

It's true he was a stubborn child.
At times he could annoy.
He can't forget one incident
From when he was a boy:

She told them not to make a "peep,"
So that's just what he said.
He got a spanking, not a laugh,
And went to cry in bed.

No matter how he tried, excelled,
He never heard, "Well done,
My son, I'm very proud of you.
To me you're number one!"

Instead, he got the putdowns
Or nothing. Which was worse?
Her hidden pain and bitterness
Had now become his curse.

But why did no adult protect
This fragile, hurting youth?
Was the silence best for him,
Or did it deny the truth?

He needed that assurance
And that protection too
From the barrage of insults
That stuck to him like glue.

A child who's injured by the one
God put there to protect
Can love, but also be confused,
Pass hurt on with the rest.

The beautiful young boy
Grew up to be a man
Who loves the Lord with all his heart,
When his hurts say he can.

He has a heart for God, we see;
It's plain to everyone,
But those who know him also know
He's hurting for someone.

He longs for her approval,
Her appreciation too.
Why can't she give agape love?
It's the godly thing to do.

It may not ever happen,
Not something she can give.
His Father tells him that's *His* love.
The man should come to Him.

God knows that he's been hurt a lot,
And it was never right.
He ought to give his pain to God.
He can take it all tonight.

He shouldn't hold on to one bit,
Or it won't go away.
He should forgive, give up all blame—
Take back his life today.

The hurting "child" suffered enough.
It shouldn't go on more.
God has great plans for this young man
That are too good to ignore.

God wants to sit and talk with him;
He has so much to tell.
If the young man follows God's advice,
He should start getting well.

God knows that we don't always
Understand the plans He makes.
He knows the future, and we don't:
Trusting Him is no mistake.

God assures the man His plans for him
Are perfect for his life.
His special gift to help him through
Is the man's unusual wife.

Though she might seem like a handful—
Too busy, not quite right—
If he treats her like God tells him,
She could be his delight.

Her disagreements—standing up
For what she thinks is real—
Are differences, not disrespect.
She's God's gift to help him heal.

God gives us what He knows we need.
We ought to understand:
Differences aren't really bad.
He created them in man.

Although her words might seem to cause
The pain he feels inside,
The pain's been there a long time now;
The devil's told him lies.

We know God's Son, while here on earth,
Was treated badly too.
His wounds can help us heal our wounds.
He's all we need. God loves you.

The Plan

··

The father he loved had to leave him early.
His death came too soon,
Leaving the young man confused and bitter.
It wasn't fair; why did he have to die like that?

The Son's death came early; the Father planned it.
It wasn't fair; why did He have to die like that?
The Father had to let his Son die
To welcome the young man's father home
And to take away the young man's confusion and bitterness.

The Father had plans for the young man,
As He had had plans for his father before him,
But the young man would never
Recognize or realize those plans,
As long as the confusion and bitterness remained.

Could he again put his trust in the Father, rather than blame him?
Could he believe in a Father whom he didn't fully understand?
Didn't he often do the same
With his other father as a child?
Isn't that what trust often involves—the unknown?

As the grief and hurt and feelings of betrayal gradually eased away,
He remembered another Son who grieved for those He loved,
Yet was betrayed.
He knew then that his father was truly home,
With the Father and Son,
And someday he would join his father
And a host of others who had believed.

Words Beat Sticks and Stones

As a child, when kids would taunt,
We told them, "Leave me be.
Sticks and stones may break my bones,
But words can never hurt me."

Since those days, we've learned the truth;
Teasing's not what we were told.
Sticks and stones may break the bones,
But words can pierce the soul.

Bumps and bruises go away.
Broken bones get strong, can heal;
But damage to a person's soul,
Though unseen, is very real.

Damage to a soul goes deep,
Affects the person's total life.
Words from others long ago
Now wound husband, kids, or wife.

Is there any way to heal
The gaping wounds that hide away,
Pouring out their poison on
Another soul another day?

To heal a life; truth is the way.
Admit the wounds, but give up blame.
Don't pass on words that wound another,
But bless them all in Jesus' name.

The Word of God can overcome
The hurt and bitterness within.
Healing and forgiveness come
When you don't pass along that sin.

Yes, sticks and stones can break your bones;
Mean words can pierce a soul.
Give up your right to hurt them back;
The Word can make you whole.

The Perfect Picture

The child should do it perfectly,
Should never do it wrong.
She learned the rules from Grandma,
Heard them her whole life long.

Her mother taught her how to clean;
Showed how to do it *right*,
Explained these were just guidelines,
Not worth getting up-tight.

She said, "See the big picture:
What's out of place, what's not.
Put up the things where they should go;
Don't fixate on one spot.

"The goal is to be tidy
Most each and every day.
Then dust and vacuum weekly
And take some time to play."

Some kids can't seem to focus;
They don't know where to start.
You give them one goal at a time,
Till they finish that small part.

"Pick up the toys on the floor;
Put them all in their place.
Put up those scattered on the bed.
Don't wash each dolly's face.

"Leave that for when you're finished,
When there is room to walk.
Do you have any questions?
When you're done, we can talk."

Why must the child still try so hard
To do it perfectly?
Procrastination often comes
When goals are hard to reach.

She hears the rules implanted
In her head so long ago,
"If your work isn't perfect,
It's not good enough to show."

Why does a grown-up harness
A child with burdens so?
Can a child reach goals an adult could not?
Does she not care or know?

Most every woman has some days
When her house is such a mess.
She's knee-deep in a project
Or trying to fix a dress.

She knows that when she's finished,
She'll clean up what she's done.
This clutter's temporary,
But not her only one.

As she's being creative,
Things scattered all around,
She's making something useful.
Her *worth* she's once more found.

She looks around and wonders
What values she's passed on.
Did her children know she loved them?
What was that love based upon?

She knew her daddy loved her,
Didn't matter what she'd done.
Then she met someone who loves her more.
He is her Father's Son.

God knows she can't be perfect.
That's His job, not her own.
He gave His life to save her
And one day bring her home.

She should teach her children of His love:
It's not for them to earn.
He gives it; they must take it.
That's all that they must learn.

It saddens God to see His flock
Try to *win* the love He's given.
They should love each other; talk with Him.
Someday they'll meet in Heaven.

Learning to Be a Man

Why does a man think
He can yell at his wife,
Just 'cause he's mad
Or upset with his life?

He barks out a list
Of each mess she's made.
Why can't she listen
To all that he's said?

He instructs her to leave
His man-cave alone.
She can do what she wants
With the rest of the home.

Never mind what it looks like
When she doesn't go in.
Empty cans, empty wrappers—
A reflection of him?

Does the daddy forget
The small ears in the house—
The child who hears all,
Remains quiet as a mouse?

What does the child think
As he curls up and hears
What is said of his mom,
Who has been brought to tears?

Is this the way
A man treats his wife?
Should he learn how to yell,
To insult, to cause strife?

He's confused. He is told
To respect Dad and Mother,
But is this what he hears,
As they "talk" to each other?

The young boy must learn
How to act like a man.
He'll be quiet, remember
Every insult he can.

For now he'll respect,
Show love to his mother,
But some day he'll grow,
Fall in love with another.

How, then, will he treat
His beautiful wife,
Whom he promises to love
For the rest of his life?

Will he love her, respect her
Like he wants to do,
Or remember Dad's actions
And "be a man" too?

Teaching Our Boys to Be Men

(A Song)

Chorus:

Do we teach our young boys
To treat a girl right
Or just how to be tough,
How to win any fight?

Is respect on the list
Of the rules we demand?
Do we show by example
How to be a real man?

Why do some men
Yell so much at their wives,
Just 'cause they are mad
Or upset with their lives?

He might bark out a list
Of mistakes she has made,
But why can't he listen
To what she just said?

He insists that she leave
His "man cave" alone.
She can do what she wants
With the rest of the home.

He leaves cans, empty wrappers
All scattered around.
His receipts, scribbled numbers
Should never be found.

Chorus

Does he even notice
His young son in the hall,
With tears in his eyes,
Trying to bounce his new ball?

What does the boy think
Of the words that he hears:
Dad belittles his mom
And brings her to tears?

Is this how a man
Should treat his young wife—
By yelling and cussing,
With insults that cause strife?

He's confused; he's been told
To respect Dad and Mother,
But that's not what he hears
As they "talk" at each other.

Chorus

The young boy tries to learn
How to act like a man—
Observes Dad to remember
Every insult he can.

For now, he'll respect
And love his sweet mother.
Wow! The new neighbor girl
Seems unlike any other.

He's not sure how to act
With his friend Betty Sue.
She reminds him of Mom,
But climbs trees with him too.

She deserves his respect
For the feats she can do—
Has a green belt in karate,
Camps out, and hikes too.

Chorus

Dad says to protect
His sister from boys;
But asks how many girls
He's "got," like they're toys.

Don't you mess with his daughter!
He will come after you.
Doesn't Dad realize
Other girls have dads too?

If the boy falls in love
With his friend Betty Sue
Or another he meets,
He must know what to do.

How then will he decide
To treat his new wife,
Whom he promises to love
For the rest of his live?

Will he love her, respect her,
Like he wants to do,
Or remember Dad's actions
And "be a man" too?

Chorus

6

Fun Poems for Our Children to Feel Special

A Valentine for My Daughter

You're my first little girl.
You're as sweet as can be.
As you're learning to grow up,
You're so special to me.

Sometimes you're good
And do everything right.
Sometimes you're not,
And we all get uptight.

You may not be perfect,
But no one can be.
Learn from your mistakes.
Be the best you can be.

Put your trust in God always.
Do what Mom and Dad say,
And you'll always be good
And sweet, like today.

Happy Valentine's Day!

(You may notice that the first child's poem in this chapter is longer than the others. That's similar to baby books. By the time there are two or more children, there is barely enough time to do all that is needed for the children, much less their baby books or their special poems. It's OK.)

Emily

You're a pretty little one,
Lots of giggles, lots of fun.
You're so sweet, my Emily.
I'm glad God sent you to me.

My Daughter

I love my little daughter.
She's cute as cute can be,
And I'm so very happy
That God sent her to me.

A Song for Karen

Little babies are so sweet.
They like to potty and they like to eat.
They like to spit up on their clothes,
But they don't like tubes sticking in their nose!

(to the tune of "Jesus Loves Me" for my third
daughter, who had a chromosome anomaly,
making it necessary to tube feed her, first
through her nose or mouth, and later with a
gastrostomy tube)

A School Prayer

Dear Lord, bless this child today,
While she works and while she plays.
Help her show your love to others,
So they can show it to their mothers.

MONIQUE – an acrostic poem

M ommy's helper

O pen and honest

N eeds hugs and love

I ntelligent, imaginative

Q uestions unending

U nderstanding beyond her years

E nergy—boundless

LIDIA – an acrostic poem

L aughter in her eyes, lots of love

I ntelligent, interesting

D aring, darling, dancing

I inquisitive

A thletic, agile, a real gem

ROGER – an acrostic poem

R unning everywhere

O ver and over—questions and movies

G ive me a hug

E yes—mischievous and beautiful

R ead to me

Belle

Once a beautiful baby, now a beautiful girl.
First she wiggled and giggled; now she sways and she twirls.
She's "as smart as a whip," loves to sing and dance too.
As a friend, she is caring; Jesus' love sure shines through.

She loves to play dress up, trying on lots of clothes.
Then she'll make up a song, poem, letter, or prose.
She is such a good student and a big sister too.
Belle's beauty starts inside, then smiles out at you.

Davis

I don't think I've met such a serious boy,
Who likes things done in specific ways.
He's amazing with puzzles, does them really fast,
Is precise in the way that he plays.

He can write his own name and copy other names too
And can build wooden planes with Granddad.
He gives detailed accounts of games that he's played,
And is the best drama king we have had.

Ezer

Once there was a cute little boy,
Who brought his mommy so much joy.
He tells a story with ease and power.
His expressions change each minute, not hour.

His imagination seems to run wild
As he makes up a tale, this quick-witted child.
He has cute chubby cheeks and a long pony tail.
We love to hear stories this funny boy tells.

7

Friendships

Ellie and Her Friends

When visiting our Bible Church,
Miss Ellie and her friend
Could really feel God's presence
From the moment they walked in.

The greeters simply smiled at them,
Shook hands, and asked their names.
God's love flowed into the visitors—
Their reactions were the same:

They knew without a doubt this was
The place God wanted them.
They went to Bible studies,
Wednesday's "Prayer and Song." Amen!

The music filled their hearts with joy.
Their prayers reached up to Heaven.
Pastor's sermons always fed their souls.
Ladies' socials gave them friends.

Ellie knew that she should use her gifts;
God had taught her what to do.
She taught classes in recovery,
From abuse, deep wounds, misuse.

At first it was a co-ed class;
That didn't last for long.
Sharing secrets in mixed company
Felt awkward and just wrong.

"Hurts, Habits, and Hang-ups" became
The new name for the class.
God brought those whom he wanted—
Healed some slow and others fast.

People came and went from group,
'Til only three remained:
Ellie and two others.
Tres Amigos they became.

Tackling boundaries, codependency,
Sharing hurts straight from the heart
Helped three introverted ladies
Learn to speak up, for a start.

God improved their self-perception,
Used their empathy and love
For each other and the hurting
To bring joy from God above.

Ellie and her buddies
Met even after class was done.
Ellie sometimes mentored one of them:
Like a mother she'd become.

The other needed a prayer partner;
Ellie said she'd take the part.
They prayed for each other's families,
And each opened up her heart.

The younger gained a new granddaughter
After she'd moved out of town,
So three *Best Buds and a Baby*
Met when the third bud was around.

Her friend's heart ached when her Daddy died;
She admired and loved that man.
He loved God, his wife, and children,
Served his church and fellowman.

Her friends were quick to comfort her.
Her pain eased; then came concern.
Ellie's strength was gone; she was depressed,
Didn't feel like leaving home.

One day, pain in her abdomen
Made Ellie go to the ER.
They removed her gall bladder easily,
But they soon found lung cancer.

Ellie loved the Lord, Almighty God,
With all her heart and soul.
When it was time to take her home,
God made her body whole.

A Belated Valentine for Ellie

Roses are red and white and pink.
God sent you as my friend, I think.
He knows what I need much better than I.
I couldn't have found you if I had tried.

God gives us friends for seasons in life
To celebrate joys and help us with strife.
He knows all your background and knows mine, too.
Together we do what He wants us to do.

I'm thankful he sent you to be my friend
And hope that our friendship will never end.
He knows His purposes and carries them through,
So I'll cherish my gift while I'm friends with you.

Hope your Valentine's Day was sweet
and the rest of the year is a blessed gift from God!

A New Friend

I haven't known her very long,
But this I know for sure—
She loves the Lord with all her heart,
And He's declared her pure.

She has a marvelous attitude
And usually wears a smile.
Her servant's heart prompts her to help;
She goes that extra mile.

She prays for others at the church
With those who meet each week.
She wants the best for those with needs;
God's answers she will seek.

She likes to do most any craft—
Make jewelry, sew, or paint.
She isn't perfect, but our God
Still sees her as a saint.

I'm glad I've come to know her
As we do our crafts together.
She's the kind of friend who's always true,
No matter what the weather.

A Masked Woman No More

The woman wore each mask just right,
So taking them off filled her with fright.
She removed each one and laid it aside
And began to see she didn't need to hide.

She was finding freedom and being real.
God had told her what was His ideal.
The stripping away had to be her choice,
To help her grasp her genuine "voice."

Peeling your layers, showing the "real you"
Is an almost impossible thing to do,
But He demands it and gives us the way
To truly relate to others each day.

Building relationships starts with truth
And includes our loyalty, like Naomi's Ruth.
When Christ's love joins two people as friends,
He's there in the storms, and as they make amends.

So, ladies, let's all remove our masks.
Freedom's worth more than simply "doing our tasks."
Can we believe how beautiful God says we are?
Or do we still try to please and seek worthless gold stars?

I believe that I heard each woman right,
As we shared our hearts in the circle that night.
We want off of the treadmill, will throw out our masks.
Would you like to join us and be real at last?

(written at a Ladies Retreat)

Walking in Her Shoes

I couldn't comprehend the pain
My friend was going through.
I'd never been where she had been
Or walked in her cute shoes.

Her muscles ached all over.
When she slept, she couldn't rest.
Fatigue made her exhausted.
Her depression took her "best."

It was hard to explain in words to us
How it ravaged her body and mind.
The symptoms of fibromyalgia
Affected her all of the time.

Depression had its hand on her;
It ruled her from day to day.
She was told to get friends who understood.
My reaction was just, "No way!"

I missed her, but could only hope
That she was doing okay.
As a Facebook friend I watched her life—
No more lunches or hugs any day.

Several years ago a friend gave me advice
That I thought I didn't much need.
I ignored getting meds for anxiety;
After crying most of one day, I took heed.

I was caring for Mom and Dad every week;
They moved through their 80s as they pleased.
My dad had dementia, couldn't do what he'd done,
But continued to smile and to tease.

Mom was a great mom for nine busy kids,
Especially with six of them boys,
But sometimes she still acts like we are not grown.
When she treats us like kids, it annoys.

Last year Daddy fell, broke his hip, and got ill
With pneumonia; he went to a home.
He got better at first, got pneumonia again.
He died. Now our mom is alone.

Mom has always enjoyed talking with anyone.
As an extrovert, it energized;
Now dementia, poor balance, and other concerns
Make it hard for her to socialize.

I take meds for anxiety now most every day,
As I help Mom one or two times per week.
More than once I have taken an emergency med,
So the things on my mind I don't speak.

As I age and realize that the crafts I enjoy
Are more often now causing my aches,
My husband mentions my RLS and my late nights
Could link to my friend's painful disease. Great!

Leticia, a Faithful Friend

We've been friends for a long time,
Since some Bible study days,
When we'd pray for those in need,
Eat good food, and chat away.

Matt would pick you up in his car.
Our group was like a family.
We learned of God from different sources,
Then you'd hitch a ride with me.

You and I've loved crafts forever—
We like to string beads on a wire,
Until we see our new creations.
We get weary, but not tired

Of seeing how our hands created
A thing of beauty from our minds.
Of course, it took all of the pieces
From friends and places of all kinds.

We both spend time making scrapbooks:
Memories of our kin and friends,
We can treasure them together,
Our crafting ideas never end.

I sometimes wonder, when I'm done
Creating some new masterpiece,
How my Creator up in Heaven
Felt when He created me.

I imagine that He belly-laughed
For all that He had done.
He gave me humor for each heartache;
He whispered how to find the fun

In situations that were unpleasant,
Out-of-control, or causing grief.
He promised me He'd always be there
To comfort me, to give relief.

One time when I couldn't sleep,
A silly picture came to mind.
God knocked down my Goliath,
Without rocks, but simple lines.

Perhaps God brought us together;
Our friendship is more than just fun.
We both lost dear ones from our families,
And did foolish things when we were young,

I've made unique cards for my family
Or for friends who're dear to me,
But you excel in your commitment
To send to friends more frequently.

I have cherished all the many
Cards you've made and sent to me,
With your words of thankfulness,
Or prayers for my family.

I know you've had a hard time lately,
As your circumstances changed.
Your body's not cooperating.
Your dreams and plans can't be the same.

I understand you have frustrations.
I have had my share of those.
I can't begin to feel the pain
You feel as those in charge say, "NO!

"You can't walk, live by yourself,
Have your own place without help."
You remember how not long ago
You did most of it yourself.

My prayer for you is that our God
Will share His "humor" gift with you.
It's served me well for all these years.
I hope that it will help you too.

Our choices make us who we are.
I'm glad I chose you as a friend.
I hope your choices move you forward.
God walks with us to the end.

Gather to Learn and Encourage

We've gathered together
And shared every heart,
But the time is soon coming
When we all must part.

Let's remember the lessons
That each woman shared
And appreciate our small groups,
As our sisters all cared.

In true joy we can go,
As new friendships may bud,
Realizing each woman
At times needs a hug.

We had fun as we learned
About each lady here—
What's her favorite color?
What household chore does she fear?

Would she hike in the mountains,
Or would she swim at the beach?
Which cuisine is her favorite?
What did all these games teach?

Though we all have our differences,
We're more alike than we know.
Do we develop new friendships,
Or to familiar pals go?

What would the woman we studied
In Proverbs 31 do?
Though industrious and wise,
She was compassionate too.

Can we possibly be
Like this strong, perfect wife?
Were her deeds simultaneous
Or done throughout her life?

Some suggest there were seasons
As she achieved every act.
That would certainly be easier,
But it's conjecture, not fact.

What we do know about her
Is she appears in God's Word.
Her nature's worth emulating—
Every trait that we've heard.

We don't have to do real estate,
Weaving, or sewing,
But live life where God puts us,
Whether coming or going.

As we go to our families,
Our homes, neighborhoods,
Can we learn to be like her,
Live as God says we should?

8

Changes

Is My Brain Trying to Rebel?

I've liked writing as far back as I can remember.
I've loved red since I was just four.
I can speak past "polite limits" from all of my memories,
But my *word recall* has a jammed door.

My brain has decided what I want to say.
Then the words jump the tracks and go hide.
I can't think of the word that I wanted to use,
And another from my lips may slide.

I am wondering if some synapses have snapped
Or the sparks that should fire have gone out.
Perhaps my late hours or some stress has stuck gears,
And in my brain I no longer have clout.

This glitch doesn't happen every day,
But at some unexpected "fun" times.
I describe what I meant or for wrong words repent,
Then explain this condition in rhyme.

Words

Excellent word recall is your friend.
You know all the words from start to the end.
You learned many words as a cute little kid,
When you labeled each item you saw, what you did.

As a teen your vocabulary is vast.
When a busy adult, you assume it will last.
Then your body slows down, and your brain does it too.
You begin to wonder what's happened to you.

You meant to say "green," but out pops "gray,"
Or you agree with someone, but tell them, "Nay"
Why are words in your brain so jumbled now?
Memories come and go, and you don't know how

To tell someone something you're trying to say.
You had the words last week, but just not today.
Memory details were vivid an hour ago,
But now all that had happened you don't even know.

You can smile and say that the words soon will come,
Or get angry, frustrated, and feel almost numb,
But that isn't helpful. You are not to blame.
These are changes that happen, but not always the same.

Each person's unique; our abilities too.
I may not have the skills to do all that you do,
But if I use my talents, helping others, do my best,
I'll find joy within me, not some words, to find rest.

Getting Older

My boobs are sagging.
My rear is dragging.
My tummy's sticking out.
My nose is sneezing.
My chest is wheezing.
It makes me want to pout.

My legs are shaking.
My meds I'm taking.
I need to pee again.
But, the Lord, He loves me,
And again He tells me
That I'm beautiful. Amen!

Allergies and Asthma Are Atrocious!

I get tired of breathing without medical aid
When cedar pollen is all through the air.
I feel like being a kid—pouting, crossing my arms.
I hate asthma. This just isn't fair.

Others have it much worse: cancer or Legionnaires.
They are dying, nothing that they can do.
I'll not think of myself, but of somebody else.
God help them. I'll keep my eyes on You.

Pity parties aren't good. They are misunderstood.
It's all wrong, and we want it all right,
But Your promises are we'll have problems and scars.
Still You're with us with all of Your might.

Lord, I wanna be well, and I know You can't tell
Me if my asthma's gonna get worse,
So I'll try to ignore when my cough's like a roar
And keep my inhaler inside my purse.

(mostly written at an urgent care place,
while fighting off bronchitis and asthma)

Turning 30 Ain't So Bad

Turning 30 ain't so bad
When you're married and a dad,
'Specially when you're never boring
To a kid who's still adoring
One he calls the best dad ever,
If not saying, "Oh! Whatever!"

And your pretty other half
Uses wit to make you laugh.
She's so glad that you're her man,
Tries to please you when she can.
Neither one's fully matured,
But your marriage has endured.

Growing old with those you love
Is a gift from God above,
Who gives comfort, wisdom, strength,
And will go to any length
To ensure His growing lad
Knows that 30 ain't so bad.

Phantom Phun on Phantom Horse

They were there as I went to my parents each week.
The large flat stones lined up so neat.
They looked like stones I've read about,
So obviously that I wanted to shout,

"Should I number them all one through ten
Or five on one and then again?"
I thought of getting my sidewalk chalk,
But I visualized something that made me balk.

Graffiti Grandma goes to jail
For numbering rocks, so she could tell
That they looked like tablets once in regard,
Now holding up dirt in someone's yard.

So I went to my desk and started to play
With the pictures of stones and the words I should say.
Writing on stones that are not my own
Is done better on paper where it's safe in my home

(These tall flat stones in front of one of the corner houses in my parents' neighborhood look like the tablets for the Ten Commandments that we have seen in the movies.)

9

Grief: My Daddy's and Best Friend's Deaths

Praying to My Father for My Dad

Why can't I talk to the One that I love
When my heart is breaking inside?
My dad has been sick in so many ways
That he said he wished he had died.

It probably seems odd that I can understand
Why he might be feeling this way.
He's always been there to take care of us;
Now can't think or just wake up some days.

He asks what he should be doing sometimes,
'Cause he knows that he previously had
His work, his chores, jobs wanted by Mom,
Tasks where all his kids needed Dad.

It should be easy to ask my Big Dad
To heal my dad when I pray,
But knowing Dad's wishes and what others want,
I'm just not sure what to say.

I told my friend, my prayer partner too,
What I thought that she should say.
She said she'd already prayed those words,
So this is what we'll pray,

"Dear Heavenly Father, you know all,
Our future and our past.
We want you to heal him, but if it's his time,
Let him go in peace and go fast."

I guess I can't tell my Heavenly Dad
What I want for my father who's here,
For I love him and want what's best for him,
But I also want him near.

So I pray to my Father; my mind starts to wander,
Trying to wait for his answer, but I know
Being quiet and still isn't easy, takes will.
To which home will God let him go?

147

My Daddy

Dad's memory was amazing,
His vocabulary vast.
Crossword puzzles were his hobby;
He'd complete them fairly fast.

He did not have bulky muscles,
But we all knew he was strong.
He'd hold one child on each hip and grin,
Made us feel we'd done no wrong.

But we knew not to do mischief,
For he'd sometimes use his belt.
He could teach us right by reason
Or by how our backsides felt.

Our dad was rather quiet,
Had to think out what he'd say.
When he spoke, we knew to listen.
We might learn some gems that day.

My dad could fix most anything,
From dolls to bikes to cars.
He built cabinets and bookcases;
His hands didn't mind the scars.

Dad was a good mechanic,
And knew engineering too.
As a carpenter, he excelled.
There's not much he couldn't do.

He could often outperform young men
Doing home repairs outside,
For he'd learned to pace himself, not rush,
With lessons he'd applied.

He had a sense of humor;
His wit was quick and dry.
He could easily get you laughing
Until you would almost cry.

Then dementia took his memory,
But not those from the past.
He could quote old songs or ditties,
Recite poems with such class.

He remembered all his family,
But not where he had been
Or where he would soon be going;
He excused it with a grin.

He thought he should be doing
Something useful as before
And would ask for our suggestions
So that he would not be bored.

Then dementia slowed his movement,
Made him shuffle more than walk,
As his muscles became weaker.
"Brain-fog" made it hard to talk.

He would get so aggravated
When his brain would not work right.
He could not think like he wanted to,
And he'd sometimes get uptight.

He tried to persevere each day
To be there for his wife.
He promised many years ago
To protect her all his life.

Then pneumonia joined dementia,
UTIs, a heart attack,
And a broken hip—together
They would thwart his bouncing back.

I knew Dad was not immortal
And some day that he would die,
But since it has finally happened,
I just feel numb and want to cry.

Knowing Dad is now in Heaven
Comforts some, but leaves the pain.
I love you, Daddy. Say "Hi" to others.
I will see you all again.

My Dad's Salvation

I asked my dad how he'd explain
Salvation to a kid,
If I would tell a grandchild,
And this is what he said,

"I began attending Sunday School
When I was five years old.
I listened to the teachers
And did what I was told,

"Believe on Jesus, and you'll be saved,
Is in John 3:16.
Then live for Him once you are His."
We discussed what all this means.

God gave us Ten Commandments
To follow as we could,
But no matter how we tried to,
We couldn't reach God's "good."

The Pharisees thought they were good;
Jesus called them "white-washed tombs."
Others asked how to be *born again*—
"Crawl back in our mothers' wombs?"

Jesus said to believe as a child does—
If God says it, it is true.
It is easy, but seems like a challenge,
Doing what Jesus said to do.

God the Father knew we were sinful
Ever since His Adam and Eve,
And we've tried to earn His approval,
But he told us to believe!

No man is perfect but His Son.
God knew that from the start.
He created us with free will;
All He asks for is our hearts.

Jesus gave His life on Calvary;
It was His Dad's plan all along.
Just accept His gift; give your life to Him—
To His family you'll belong.

God doesn't use a big eraser
Each time we are not good,
To erase us from the Book of Life.
We repent; He sees Jesus' blood.

Not one of us can win God's love
By our deeds or by our prayers.
He loves us when we're still in sin,
But doesn't want us to stay there.

He has wooed us with His Spirit,
Sent His *angels* we call *friends*.
Jesus gave His life so we could live
With Him, when we make amends.

Christianity's not a religion;
It's a relationship with Him.
His Son taught about the Father's love
And wants to see us all in Heaven.

He wants everyone to come to Him,
For He loves us as we are.
Through His Spirit you become like His Son
When you accept His life, His scars.

Dad believed in Jesus and was saved,
Then lived his life to show
He loved the Lord with all his heart,
His mind, his very soul.

He loved his neighbors as himself;
Helping others made him glad.
Now he's up in Heaven with his Lord.
I'll see you someday, Dad.

Father God, HELP! Sometimes Grief Just Stinks

Father God, I want to scream;
I'm hurting deep inside.
My best friend and my Daddy,
Whom I loved so much, have died.

My Daddy understood and cared
Though his memory was gone.
He loved me as he always had;
For him my heart still longs.

When my head got above water,
As I almost drowned from grief,
Then my friend died much too quickly,
And my heart needs some relief.

I no longer have sweet Ellie
When the pain's too much to bear,
For I talked to her of Daddy,
Asking for her help in prayer.

I know I need to turn to You
When my losses I can't bear,
But it's so much easier to hear You
If You're near me in a chair.

I need to hear the words aloud,
To feel Your warm embrace.
I can only hold the tears so long
Till they're streaming down my face.

Help my brain turn off when it's time to rest;
And take sleep aids when I should,
At appropriate times, before it's too late.
Staying up all night's not good.

I may feel like I need to cry, but can't,
Or I'll weep at ridiculous times.
I'll keep trying to say what I need to say
In these desperate, awkward rhymes.

I know others are worse off than me,
And their livelihood's at stake,
But my house, my food, and the clothes I wear
Cannot take away the ache.

My husband wants to help me,
But he doesn't know what to do,
And I'm not even sure that I know,
So I'm giving it all to You.

When You're in a Fog, Look to the Light

I moved in slow motion
As I trudged through the fog.
I drank coffee, made small talk,
And played with the dog.

I was lucky a light
Penetrated the mist,
As I abruptly remembered
My day's to-do list.

Mom needed new glasses;
My job was to drive.
So I got it in gear,
And my brain came alive.

I finished my coffee,
Took a shower, and got dressed,
Forgot to take meds,
But I did all the rest.

Mom was early, not late,
So we got the job done.
Zooming zero to sixty,
Fog to frenzy's no fun.

The haze seems self-made,
But it wasn't conceived
In my brain's consciousness,
Or that's what I believe.

Maybe hidden inside
The brain's small inner core
Is a room where our anguish
Hides behind guarded doors.

We do not want the pain
That it brings to our souls,
So we keep the doors locked,
But we never feel whole.

We are taught the best way
Is to open doors slow—
Let a little out, deal with it,
Move through the rows

Of memories made
With the loved ones we lost,
For if we don't confront them,
We could pay a high cost.

Over time counselors learned
Stuffing pain deep inside
Makes hurts seep or spew out
At times we don't decide.

We must deal with each memory
Until we can smile
Through the tears that we cry,
But it may take a while.

Some suggest we rely
On a buddy who cares,
To walk with us through grief;
But my buddy's not there.

She's not at her house,
For she's gone to her Home.
I've lost Daddy, now her,
And I feel so alone.

In truth, I'm surrounded
By family and friends.
Those wanting to help
Don't know where to begin.

I don't know what to say;
I don't know how I feel.
I'm just numb, in a daydream,
And I wish this weren't real.

But my loved ones are gone;
They'll never return,
So I creep through my grief,
Cry or weep at each turn.

The best one to turn to
In hard times like these
Is the One who's been there
As His Father He pleased.

Though pure, He was hung
On the cross for our sins.
Scourged and beat, He knew pain;
He did not hold it in.

He cried out to His Father
When His Dad turned His face;
He can comfort us now
And light up our dark place.

Then Jesus spoke to them again,
saying, "I am the light of the world.
He who follows Me shall not walk in
*darkness, but have the **light** of life."*
(John 8:12, NKJV)

My Grief Journey—Jolts, Justice, and Just Plain Awesome!

I have grieved till I am goofy;
I have cried until I'm dry.
I had emotions, ever-changing,
Without always knowing why.

I would feel the urge to cry,
But I couldn't, so I'd frown;
Or my feelings just seemed frozen,
Then zoomed up or tumbled down.

What I've learned as I've been grieving
For my daddy and best friend
Is the deep love I had for them
Continues on; it never ends.

Sudden death, for any reason,
Takes a toll on those who're left,
Like disorders some called "lethal"—
Either way, you are bereft.

Knowing Dad accepted Jesus,
When he was just a child of five,
Gives me joy, peace, and comfort.
With our Lord, my dad's alive.

Ellie also loved our Savior
And is probably giving hugs
To her Jesus, all the angels,
And the whole host up above.

My sweet baby with Trisomy,
Went to Heaven with our Lord.
Though we miss her, she is healed now,
And we'll meet at Heaven's door.

I am not afraid of death,
For I know whom I'll see then:
Father God, His Son, and Spirit,
All my loved ones and saved friends.

Through my grief, I've learned my limits
And learned how far God extends
All the gifts bestowed upon me
To help others, comfort them.

God loves us and gives us comfort;
And that's what he asks of us.
Have compassion for the hurting;
Demonstrate to them God's love.

That big hole that's in our heart now
Is the one God made for Him.
He alone can truly fill it
With His peace, His love, His vim.

We first learned about our Jesus
In the Bible and kids' songs:
Jesus loves me, loves all children,
Even when we're doing wrong.

With joy we ought to take God's present
That He offers to us all—
His Son Jesus' substitution
On the cross for mankind's fall.

Jesus said He is the Way;
He is also Heaven's door.
Getting to the Father through Him,
Is what He asks, and nothing more.

*[God] who comforts us in all our troubles,
so that we can comfort those in any trouble
with the comfort we ourselves receive from
God.* (2 Corinthians 1:4 NIV)

*But God demonstrates his own love for us in
this: While we were still sinners, Christ died
for us.* (Romans 5:8 NIV)

*For it is by grace you have been saved,
through faith—and this is not from yourselves,
it is the gift of God—not by works, so that no
one can boast.* (Ephesians 2:8-9 NIV)

Alone, or Not?

Why do I feel so all alone
When there're people all around?
Why do I feel they don't hear a word
When I utter every sound?

Is that how my Lord felt that fateful night
When He took His hand-picked men
To the garden to pray, while He prayed alone?
They could not stay awake till the end.

Did they not understand He desired their support,
As He wrestled with His own human fear?
He was asking His Father if His death must still come,
And He wanted His beloved friends near.

My dearest sweet friend is no longer on earth,
But is with our Lord up above.
With whom do I now share the depths of my soul,
But my God and the family I love?

I can talk to my husband and daughters,
But some thoughts are best told to a friend.
God created girls to need friendships.
Our deep thoughts just might frighten our men.

10

Grief: My Younger Brother Steve's Death

Wanted: Good Assistant for Mr. Young

Steve says that Heaven's "perfect."
Dad was called there by the Lord
To help fix things now aging,
So they can be restored.

The Pearly Gates had just begun
To creak and show some rust.
The toasters and the blenders
Needed fixed by a man God could trust.

Dad's a whiz at tweaking antennas,
So radios and TVs work right,
And he learned keeping toilets unclogged
Prevented messy repairs at night.

He can square up legs on tables
So they never wobble again.
Dad can fix most any appliance,
But the workload's too much for one man.

So the Good Lord looked over all His lists,
Finally asked for suggestions from Dad.
Now he'll soon have a worthy assistant,
Although it will make the rest of us sad.

(When Dad died, Steve wrote a humorous poem
explaining that God must have called Dad to
Heaven to keep things working well up there. His
idea was focused on Dad's ability to fix most anything,
not Heaven's actual need to have anything fixed.
This is my poem to explain why Steve joined Dad.)

The Many Faces of Steve

···

When Steve was born in '52,
I had not yet turned three,
But I knew this baby coming home
Was a special gift for me.

We'd play with dollies or stack blocks,
Once he could move around;
Then push some cars across the floor
Or pull grass from the ground.

We lived out in the country,
Wore our underwear outside.
Little girls did not need t-shirts then,
But, oh, how time just flies!

Our dress codes have all changed now,
So has the way we play.
We didn't need to plug in toys
Like most kids do today.

On our old teeter-totter,
We'd hang down from the bars,
Pretend to swing and go somewhere,
Though we couldn't go too far.

Little Steve was such a cute boy.
His smile lit up the place.
He could be shy and quiet,
Or might brighten your whole day.

While Stan and I attended school,
And spent time with our friends,
Steve stayed home, made up his own.
Imagination has no end.

Steve could be so curious,
Found a drawer of Stanton's stuff.
Stan nailed the drawer up in a tree
When he had climbed high enough.

That didn't stop our little Steve,
At least not much at first,
For he climbed up in the tree to look,
But saw going down was worse.

Mom came out and coaxed him down,
Made Stan bring down the drawer,
But I never knew if little Steve tried
Such a fool stunt anymore.

When the family moved to Bellaire,
And Steve knew no one yet,
His class got cupcakes from the principal;
Steve's birthday was a hit.

Steve once was made drum major
In our church school's bagpipe band,
But his very favorite thing to do
Was to travel across the land.

We both enjoyed riding our bikes,
But he desired to do more.
Motorcycles went much faster:
The world he could explore.

He has driven out to Big Bend
And has traveled to Mexico.
He's been all over Texas
And places I don't even know.

Steve's had smaller bikes and large ones:
Harleys, Hondas, other brands.
He's hauled tents or pop-up trailers
And camped throughout the land.

He rode alone, with brothers,
And maybe with some friends.
His time exploring this country
Has now come to an end.

Steve was quite the poet—
Wrote of people he had known:
Some kids who grew up, some who didn't,
One who'd hardened as she'd grown.

He wrote of special women
Whom he'd met both near and far,
Captured their beauty with his pen—
That trait that set them apart.

He could write political satire,
And a limerick or two.
But his portrayals of kids and women
Could make their souls shine through.

When the family moved to Austin,
Steve stayed to watch their home.
I had recently been married,
Mom and Dad said we could come.

We'd move into the house they left,
Pay them rent, start our new life.
We would clean it, paint it, fix it up.
Steve would stay for just a while.

Somehow the plans changed easily,
Jen was born in '79.
Within two years, her dad moved out,
So Steve stayed; I didn't mind.

I was a working, single mom.
Steve watched Jen; I was blessed.
He played with her, looked after her;
She thought he was the best.

He was there when Jen first stood up
By herself, as a photo shows.
He loved animals and children;
He even got our dogs to pose.

But life is full of changes.
I remarried, moved away.
Then I had two other children.
I was busy every day.

Steve got married, had a son.
I didn't see him near as much,
But I've always loved him dearly,
Even when we weren't in touch.

My kids married; I'm a Nana,
And Steve loved my grandkids too.
Now you're with our Dad in Heaven,
But I'm down here missing you.

My Grief Is Not Always Friendly

You said that you don't like it
When I'm acting so depressed.
Do you wonder why it's happening?
I don't like being such a mess!

As you recall, my brother died
About six weeks ago.
Depression, anger, sadness
Are all part of grief, you know.

Withdrawing from your partner
Or from others whom you love
Is not all that uncommon.
Then I also had to move!

Steve died on April twenty.
Our house flooded May thirteen.
Three weeks is hardly time to grieve.
Instead, I've packed, unpacked, and cleaned.

Some days I'm drowning in my sorrow,
But I may not even know.
If you threw a life preserver,
Would I grab it, then let go?

What I need is understanding.
I've lost my brother and my home.
If my mood is not too friendly,
I may need to be alone.

I keep busy when I'm hurting.
If I slow down, I will cry.
I can't handle some discussions.
My brain crashes when I try.

Please don't try to reason with me.
By brain's somewhere in a fog.
My emotions are so raw now,
I can barely pet our dog.

I remember when you told me
That grief sometimes may take years.
Your friend had died three years earlier,
But his memory could still bring tears.

That's the reason I watch comedy.
I need laughter so I'll heal.
I don't act this way on purpose.
Grief affects the way I feel.

I Don't Want the Pain

Why do I sometimes wish I were gone?
I just want to stop all the pain.
I miss my brother, my dad, and my friend—
Their deaths make my tears fall like rain.

Some days I'm numb and just want to sleep.
Other times I can barely sit still.
Those days I really get a lot done;
The next day I don't know how I feel.

Grief is not easy; it never has been,
But we don't have to walk it alone.
God sent us His Son to walk by our side
Through the valleys until we go Home.

Sometimes I want shortcuts; I don't want to hurt,
But it's not my decision to make.
God gave me my life to live for Him now.
Trying to end it would be a mistake.

I don't want to hurt all my family and friends.
How can I stop the pain deep inside?
I know grief is a journey that we must go through.
If we don't, all the pain simply hides.

When we least expect it, it rears its mean head:
We get angry and scream who knows what,
Or break into tears as we drive down the road,
And have no idea what caused all of that.

Am I ready to give up my life to stop pain?
Give that pain to the ones whom I love?
What a selfish decision to consider at all!
Our pain was placed on the Son up above.

We'll all have sorrow and suffering at times;
In God's Word it says that it's true.
If I want to get rid of all of my pain,
Why would I wish to dump it on you?

"Why me?" is a question we may ask at times,
But the answer we already know.
God lets things occur: others have free will too.
He decides when we stay, when we go!

Grief Can Hurt

Grief is such a fickle thing.
It toys with your emotions.
Just when you think you're doing fine,
It causes a commotion.

It makes you feel your life's not worth
What you once thought it was.
It questions all your values—
Smacks your brain waves till they buzz.

It jolts your nerves until you can't
Calm them for quite a while.
You need to cry, can't be consoled.
You cannot even smile.

I hate the way it makes me feel,
Know God can help me, if He will.
I need to sleep, to just be still.
God whispers that I am His, for real.

My life's not worthless, not to Him,
Or to my friends or family.
I should ignore Grief's gloomy words.
I need the truth, which sets me free.

I should calm myself and get some rest.
Tomorrow's light reveals what's true.
The darkness I've walked through to heal
Reminds me of what God's brought me through.

Though Grief can creep up in the dark
And make me think of all my strife,
My Father's Light will soon reveal
The value of my precious life.

*So they sat down with him on the ground seven days and seven nights, and no one spoke a word to him, for they saw that his **grief** was very great.* (Job 2:13 NKJV)

*But I would strengthen you with my mouth, And the comfort of my lips would relieve your **grief**.* (Job 16:5 NKJV)
[Job said this to his friends, as if he were speaking to them in their grief, for their words were not comforting to him in his grief.]

*Have mercy on me, O Lord, for I am in trouble; My eye wastes away with **grief**, Yes, my soul and my body!* (Psalm 31:9 NKJV)

*For I will turn their **mourning** into joy, and comfort them, and give them joy for their sorrow.* (Jeremiah 31:13 NASB)

For He Himself has said, "I will never leave you nor forsake you." (Hebrews 13:5b NKJV)

The Spirit Himself bears witness with our spirit that we are children of God. (Romans 8:16 NKJV)

*Come to me, all you who are weary and burdened, and I will give you **rest**.* (Matthew 11:28 NET)

Then Jesus spoke to them again, saying, "I am the light of the world. He who follows Me shall not walk in darkness, but have the light of life." (John 8:12 NKJV)

Then Jesus said to those Jews who believed Him, "If you abide in My word, you are My disciples indeed. And you shall know the truth, and the truth shall make you free." (John 8:31-32. NKJV)

Dispelling the Darkness

There's a cloud that comes over me once in a while
That brings with it darkness and dread.
Although I'm not trying to make it appear,
Some might say it's all in my head.

When it's late and I just can't get ready for bed,
And I really have no idea why,
It creeps up behind me and snatches my joy.
Then I feel that I simply must cry.

Other times when I'm getting up late in the morn
'Cause I stayed up the night before late,
My feet feel like lead, and there's fog in my head.
Until coffee, the day has to wait.

I may start out thinking I merely am tired,
But then, suddenly, I need to cry,
But the pain and heaviness deep in my heart
Can produce not a tear in my eye.

I decide to the doctor I'll go for advice.
By the time I am ready to call,
The cloud's lifted and gone to find somebody else
To pester; I'm not sad at all.

My joy's come back, though it never was gone.
It was hidden, waiting for me to seek.
When I look to the Light, darkness cannot abide.
He is strongest when I realize I'm weak.

Depression and Its Abuse

Depression is a liar
Who comes after you and me.
Your skin tone doesn't matter;
He doesn't want you free.

Enslaving is his pastime;
You think that you are not.
He lies to you of freedom,
Until he's sure you're caught.

Depression is a killer.
The more worthless that you feel
Will give him overconfidence
That you will do his will.

Depression's very powerful,
Can throw caution to the wind.
You cower in fear, but he just sneers,
As he tells you that you've sinned.

He doesn't care for reasons,
'Cause any one will do.
His goal's your isolation,
Till his loathing's eaten you.

He tells you you're not worthy.
Everything is all your fault.
A dark cloud overshadows you;
Your progress seems to halt.

Depression isn't easy.
It comes and goes at will.
Are you really moving forward,
Or are you standing still?

Depression can't be predicted.
Effects aren't the same for all.
The pill and counselor that help me
May not help you at all.

If there's Hell, Depression lives there,
Makes you feel you live there too:
Brings up your past, can make it last,
Till you don't know what to do.

Depression can cause darkness
So thick you can hardly breathe.
When you fall straight to the bottom,
Remember the truths you believe.

In a panic I say like a "mantra"
(Though I'm really not sure what that is)
Words I've heard many times from the Good Book.
On the brink, do I jump, do I live?

Once my pastor and counselor asked me,
"Do you know that you're on the brink
Of a serious nervous breakdown?"
I said, "Yes, but here's what I think:

"I can see o'er the edge, but can't jump now.
Escaping's a luxury I can't afford.
I must care for my beautiful children."
Then I say over and over these words:

For God has not given [me] a spirit of fear, but
of power and of love and of a sound mind.
(2 Timothy 1:7 NKJV)

(I don't know about others who feel like they are on the
brink of a nervous breakdown, but in that moment, I really
need a sound mind.)

Our Grief Facilitators

Our leader's not invincible,
But she knows what to do,
When you feel like your whole world
Is crashing down on top of you.

It's not that she's an expert,
But she's been there before.
The loss of her dear loved one
Prepared her to comfort more.

This group is not the kind
For which we line up to enroll,
But rather we seek help for grief
When death's taken its toll.

We're on a voyage we didn't pick;
We need someone to guide us.
That's what facilitators do
But their aim's not to provide us

With a simple list of do's and don'ts.
That isn't how grief works.
It's tailored to each one of us,
How deep our love, how hard our hurt.

We're grateful for the comfort
And the guidance she provides,
And thankful for the insight
With which she's enriched our lives.

Wanda's been a leader of
Our close-knit grieving group.
Don has added his perception
Of how grief affects men too.

Whether death has snatched a spouse,
Parent, child, sibling, or friend,
We've learned to turn to Jesus;
He can guide us to the end.

Our journey may be long in years,
But it's one we must go through.
With our leaders, friends, and Savior
Steering, knowing what to do,

We'll come out of our dark tunnel,
And we'll step into the light.
We will thank all those who helped us
Run the race, fight the good fight.

Thank you, facilitators, for
your guidance on our journeys.

— 11 —

Grief: My Mom's Death

A Mom's Love

Mom taught me about love—
Not with long flowery words,
But by pouring herself a cup of tea
And drinking it in her room,
By herself, except for her tears.

Mom had just swept and mopped the living room.
The cement floor still had no covering.
Dad built the house, but it wasn't quite finished.
Their young children tried to help.
Ajax found all the cement cracks and dents.

Mom drank her tea.
She probably prayed or read.
She cleaned the floor once more,
And maybe told us not to use Ajax again.
I told myself not to do that again.
I didn't like to see my Mom sad.

Mom and Dad took us on regular vacations.
We visited people in Mama's family.
We could tell she loved them, and they loved her.
We heard happy, excited, caring words.
We saw love in action.

We soon loved these people too.
They were family.
Miles didn't matter.
Being together did.

Mom showed us how to be creative.
We got really messy,
Putting newspaper strips in flour and water.
We blew up balloons to different sizes.
Then we smeared that paper all over the balloons,
Until Mom said, "That's enough."

The hardest part began:
Waiting for wet paper to dry.
We probably ran and played outside
To release the pent-up "waiting" energy.
Mom took the time to show us
How to do the things she loved—
Being creative in so many ways.

When the paper was dry,
We popped the balloons inside.
It was time to design our puppet heads—
Faces, hair, accessories.
Mom made most of the costumes
And showed some of us how.
Our messy play was over.
The puppet shows began.
Mom helped us with those too.

As an only child,
Mom had no experience helping with babies.
After her first child was born,
She learned that her husband knew nothing
About taking care of babies either,
Even though he had five siblings.
He had helped his dad, not his mom.

She asked her mom for some advice,
But long distance calls were expensive.
Letters weren't usually fast enough.
She asked the pediatrician how to help a sick child.
She asked God how to train a child.
She gradually learned how to care for her new son.

Mom looked for guidance in God's Word.
God loved David unconditionally and was there for him.
David loved God, talked to him, and trusted him.
Mom would love, protect, and support her children the same way,
Until the little ones knew they could trust her.
She would speak to her children and teach them about God.
Listening to people and God was harder for her,
But she was learning that too.

Mom read about God's promise
To give his people a beautiful, bountiful home.
Moses was the leader,
But he, too, had to learn.
God got his attention with a burning bush.
God got Mom's attention with her beautiful baby boy,
Who wouldn't stop crying.

"What have I gotten myself into?"
Was Mom's first big question.
As she learned answers for herself,
She also helped her children learn
How to find the answers to their own questions.

While Moses tried to convince God
To get someone more qualified for the job of leader,
Mom did her best to become more qualified
For her new job as Mother.
She was determined, even tenacious.
"A job worth doing is worth doing right."

God told Moses to quit whining,
That he was going to do the job anyway.
His brother would help him.
Sometimes Mom told us to quit whining
About the task she had assigned to us
If we wanted any help at all
And didn't want to get into more trouble.

She usually made sure, somehow,
That we knew how to do the job "right."
Sometimes it was through on-the-job training.
Other times it started with, "Go to my room.
We need to talk."
As much as some of us didn't like the talks,
She did try to explain what we should do,
What we did wrong, or what we had avoided doing.
That is love too.

Perhaps God got Mom's attention
When she was reading verses like Proverbs 29:17.
Her King James Version was different,
But the Contemporary English Version says:
"If you correct your children,
They will bring you peace and happiness."
What's a mother not to love about that?

As each of her children became a teenager, or preteen,
She faced new challenges.
Each of us could come up with a different version
Of the game: "101 Ways to Provoke Your Parents."
Even before the internet, parents had networking systems.
They had books, family, friends, pastors, priests, or neighbors.
Mom didn't always respond to our antics as we expected,
But she would respond.

She told one son that if he wanted to climb the mall's light pole again
With his friends, at least have her there, too.
Then she could call EMS if one of them fell.
Later she watched that same son fly through the air
As a gymnast on the high bar, parallel bars, the vault,
And any other way he could dangerously be in midair.

She gave her blessing to one of her sons
Who loved to ride off on his motorcycle,
Either with family or friends or all by himself,
To places far away, in or out of our country.
He loved it. She loved him. She prayed,
As she had for the son who loved being up high
In midair, with nothing to hold onto.
She knew whose hands were nearby
To help them when she couldn't.

Mom was not always calm,
Any more than her teen and young adult kids,
But we always knew we could eventually talk.
Sometimes neither Mom nor kids listened, not completely,
But the lines of communication were always there.
Love needs communication.

Mom and Dad loved each other.
He was her handsome Marine,
He thought she was beautiful
From the time he first saw her.

They didn't show their love to each other
In the same way,
But they would still hold hands sometimes,
Even in their eighties and nineties.
Mom helped Dad through his years of dementia.
He still tried to take care of her as much as he could.
Mom talked about her feelings.
Dad didn't. He acted on his feelings.

It amazes me today how much all of us
Still love and even like each other and get along.
There are only eight of the nine now,
But we enjoy each other's company.
We laugh together.
We cry together.
We cried when Dad left us.
We cried when she joined him.

Mom, we love you now and forever.

Dear Husband

You comfort me when I am down
And do it with a smile.
You know that since my mama died,
I'll be hurting for a while.

My moods can swing from high to low;
You offer me a drink.
You fix me food or bring a snack.
I seem close to the brink.

It's not the first time I've been there,
Nor will it be the last.
You gently urge me from the edge—
Memories pop up from my past.

Our anniversary had to wait.
You told me not to worry.
Jen took me to the hospital.
We thought we'd better hurry.

With kids and grandkids by her side,
Mom took her final breath.
Our pain was overwhelming.
She's no longer here on earth.

I loved my mom, knew it was time,
But it hurt to see her go.
Her memory's back, her beauty too.
My pain's begun, I know.

I've been through grief, don't like it much,
But I know that I must go.
The journey's mine, but I'm not alone.
Your hand's near mine, I know.

Thank you for being there when I need it
most—for thirty awesome years.

(Our anniversary was shortly after Mom's death.
I wrote this several days after our anniversary.)

Mom's Death, My Reactions

I realized I'd built some walls
To keep me safe. They wouldn't give.
I know I have to take a step
Outside those walls for me to "live."

Being strong, holding it all in
May seem like the right move at first,
But eventually the walls will not last.
My emotions will scream to be heard.

I feel that I must try to cry,
But nothing I do will bring the tears.
I look at her photos, read her stories.
All I see are her dying fears.

I can't get the picture out of my head
Of Mom looking afraid to go.
Did I really see fear? Was it normal for death?
Was I right or wrong? I don't know.

We tried to calm her, touched her forehead,
Told her it was her time to go.
She'd soon be with Jesus, family, and friends.
She loved her Lord, I know.

Mom would talk about being "good enough,"
Final cramming to get into Heaven,
But our "good works" don't work;
We are saved by our faith.
God's love and His grace get us in.

I've seen people die, but not like my mom.
Was my perception a mere illusion?
My walls are still here, and there's barely a tear.
My mom's death has just brought me confusion.

Family

....

Mom lived her life for her family.
She'd seen it done all of her life.
The Depression brought families together.
Where there's love, it can minimize strife.

As a baby she lived with grandparents,
Aunts, uncles, her mom, and her dad.
Some would leave to find jobs, find love, something else;
They did their best with the training they had.

Mom's dad found most of his work out of town.
She didn't know why he couldn't be home.
Understanding his need to support his two girls
Was too hard when her daddy was gone.

Mom saw all the ways this large family worked.
Guy and Maude helped their kids when they could.
Grown kids paid back loans when they made it back home.
Those at home did the chores that they should.

Family members were usually busy
At a job, fixing food, cleaning house.
Mom saw siblings all helping each other.
Kids helped parents; grandparents helped out.

Mom learned her work ethic from watching:
Learned to cook and sew from different ones.
When the chores were all done, they'd play music,
Sing along or play cards—just have fun.

Mom met her handsome Marine in DC.
They got married and moved to the South.
Their first son gave them the realization
Neither knew how to quiet his mouth.

Babies cry for a myriad of reasons.
They're hungry, messed a diaper, have gas.
The young couple asked everyone questions.
They needed baby care answers and fast.

Mom didn't have family in Houston,
Except those related to Dad.
She made a list of role models and helpers,
The best list a new mom ever had.

Her new baby helped her learn a lesson:
Stay in touch with your family and friends.
They're a resource, companion, a buddy;
Your need for their love never ends.

Mom and Dad taught us valuable wisdom,
Disguised as scolding, lectures, discipline.
We were blessed with our godly ancestors,
Whose love turned out loving women and men.

The Notebook Lesson

....

I saw the movie, "Notebook,"
For about the third time now.
Each time the end surprises me.
I don't remember it somehow.

I watched it since tears wouldn't come,
Though Mom recently had died.
I cried, but something shocked me:
Mom and Dad's love came alive.

Dad loved Mom when he first saw her.
Mom saw a well-bred, handsome Marine.
He called her after he left DC
And asked her to wear his ring.

He fixed radios on fighter planes
On an island in the Pacific.
She was 16, finishing high school,
Adored her ring. He's so terrific!

He married the beautiful love of his life
When his salary was enough for her dad.
He moved her to Texas, way down in the South.
The shock to her systems was bad.

Her ideals of how in-laws would treat her
Was reality-checked right away,
But her fighting determination
Proved to all that she *was* here to stay.

He had made a commitment to love her
And take care of her all of his life.
She would do all she could for her family,
While proving she's one sweet, sexy wife.

The Marine and his bride made some babies.
When they finally stopped, there were nine.
Though they showed love in ways that were different,
Their eyes said their romance was fine.

She loved doing crafts with her children.
They would all go on vacations too.
He spent time by himself fixing cars and what else,
But they'd all do what she liked to do.

They made God a big part of the family—
Went to church, served in ways that they could,
Sent their kids to a church school in Houston,
Tried to model what God says is good.

As the kids grew and had their own interests,
Mom and Dad found their own interests too.
They would visit museums of all sorts,
Learn of family, and go on a cruise.

Mom would try to get Dad to go dancing.
Watching musicians play had to do.
They liked a variety of music.
Now their children all like music too.

At his 90th birthday she shocked him—
Did a belly dance, sat in his lap.
While their family and friends in disbelief stared,
Stifling laughter. Did she think they should clap?

We had recently seen Mom and Dad holding hands,
Look with love into each other's eyes,
But this couple, though old, showed us they were still bold.
Their kids couldn't outdo their surprise.

My Tears

I wonder what's going on in my head.
I think that my "cry" switch is stuck.
I try switching it on, but the poor tears won't come.
Have the fog and the cobwebs made muck?

I watch some sad movies; I'm sure that will work,
But the tears are as scarce as before.
I read some grief poems I wrote years ago.
Maybe something has padlocked the door.

Most men's brains have compartments and doors to each one.
They can open and shut them at will.
My brain's doors were split and stayed open on top.
All the rooms shared their data until . . .

Mom got sick and then died with family there.
Kids and grandkids tried to ease her trip "home."
We did not act the same; I sat and stared at it all.
The person dying in bed wasn't "Mom."

My thoughts would make no sense to those in the room
Who saw her body get worse, her life go.
Something inside my brain saw how intense my pain.
It then decreased the grief pain I'd know.

I learned of grief with the death of my baby.
When Dad died, I lived through it again.
My brother's death hurt; he helped raise my first girl.
Now that Mom died, shock has hidden the pain.

Mom helped her kids discover their interests.
She led Brownies and Scouts and much more.
She got library books into our neighborhood.
She drove and sewed till my mom I adored.

Mom had talents she shared with her children.
She loved reading and creative expression.
She played music—we danced, moved our bodies around.
Being a mom was her favorite profession.

As a child I tried to be "Mommy's Helper."
She had too much work with so many kids.
Later she said, "Skip the laundry and dishes;
Make sure that your children are His."

Mom and Dad taught us love was important.
He used actions; she preferred using words.
They both lived a long time; he loved puns; she loved rhyme.
When our grief turns to joy, 'twill be heard.

As I look back at all that I've written,
I think I'm beginning to see
That the love that I had for my mom and my dad
Has left pain overwhelming for me.

My brain's trying to regulate sorrow.
I watched Mom leave before she had died.
The pain must ease out slow, there's so much; now I know
Why I stopped short whenever I cried.

Mom and Me

I know Mom loved me in my head,
Not in my fragile heart.
Dad loved me unconditionally.
I felt it from the start.

Mom had no siblings, just an aunt,
Who was older by six years.
Their extended families shared a home
During the Depression there.

When Mom was young, her dad was gone
To find jobs where he could.
She wondered if he loved her.
He wrote letters saying he did.

Mom's mom worked several different jobs
At a hospital in town.
She also sang in their church choirs.
Mom had other family around.

Later, when her dad was finally home,
He worked nights, slept in the day.
Mom knew better than to wake him up.
Her friends had to stay away.

Mom met her Marine when just 16.
Then he left DC for the War.
They were married two years later.
He had been worth waiting for.

When their first child came, she asked the Lord
How to take care of their son.
She'd use God's Fatherly example
Of Love and Discipline.

When three, I wanted to help my mom,
But didn't know what to do.
We put Ajax on her concrete floor.
She was sad, not saying, "Thank you."

When my new baby sister cried in her crib,
Mom was in the bathroom; Dad was gone.
At nine, I knew I could help my Mom.
My sister wasn't crying for long.

Mom asked me why the crying had stopped.
I told. She said, "Sit on the bed."
She explained that Sis was too wiggly.
She feared I'd drop her on her head.

Mom must have seen that I liked to dance.
She got me lessons when I was but three.
I started weekly lessons when I was eight.
When I danced, I felt finally like *me*.

I was "rain," as I did my jazz solo.
I twirled in red the next year, now en pointe.
I did adagio with the most handsome partner.
Our family moved; there was no time; "What was the point?"

I wasn't a lot like my momma.
I was a little bit more like my dad.
I was shy (not at home), full of questions, not like some.
I could potentially have driven her mad.

As I think of the things Momma taught us—
Love for music, dance and reading, play and fun,
Love for God, family, friends, and the needy—
It's plain to see all the good she has done.

She put her heart into her kids as we grew up.
She did without so we would have what we'd need.
Without kids there, Dad built a second closet.
She bought and sewed clothes for *her*. She was free!

Mom and Dad then had time for each other.
They heard Ed Miller, bagpipe players, and more.
They toured museums and studied family histories,
Then enjoyed dinners for two, no longer more.

When Mom was 90, she was diagnosed with dementia.
To our surprise, we learned she had ADHD.
It made sense then—things she had done and not done.
She did the best for us she could, even for me.

— 12 —

Our Legacy—a Family's Faith, Love for Learning, and Penning of Poetry

The following poems are not my poems, but were written by seven generations of my family. Beginning in 2007, when I was helping Mom in Houston after she broke her femur, I began looking at our family's history in more detail—not simply pedigree charts, but the personal stories about numerous ancestors. They became as "real" to me as they had been to my grandma and mom, not merely words and photos on a page. Mom began giving me many of the ancestry records, photos, documents, letters, and miscellaneous papers. Those included some poetry. I began to scan and digitize as much of the material as I could to share with family. I am still organizing the papers and photos in my office. Now I have decided to share a few of their poems with you, the reader. Additionally, after talking to people in my family about adding this new chapter to the book, some of them decided to share their work, as well. Enjoy!

- The first two poems are by Corinia Maria Grover Mack, my 3rd great-grandmother. She lived from 1830 to 1930 and celebrated her 100th birthday before her death. Her husband fought in the Civil War. While he was gone, she supported herself and her children with her skills as a seamstress and a milliner (one who makes hats). Most of the clothes which remained (out of all of the elegant garments she had made) have been sent to a museum. At the age of 60, Corinia learned German. I found a letter she had written entirely in German among her papers. I am not sure who she wrote the included poems for, but her love for those people and her faith are evident.

- The second two are by Corrie Geneva "Jennie" Mack Webster, Corinia and Israel Mack's daughter. She was my 2nd great-grandmother. She wrote one poem about Lucy Rolph Grover, her mom's mother. The other poem was for Katie E. Bulfinch, the younger sister of her husband, Melvin Harvey Webster. Katie was only 31 when she died, and her saved funeral card reveals that she died on March 3, 1890. Jennie's faith was also clear, as well as her fondness and love for Katie.

- The next poem is by my great-grandmother, Maude Webster Brown, who was married to Guy Benjamin Brown. She was apparently concerned that her daughter, Ethlyn, might have difficulty writing about Santa for a school assignment. It appeared to be during World War I, which was causing Santa great difficulty in accessing his toys or the parts for them for all the children of the world. Maude, lovingly called "Baba," fixed the problem, at least in her poem.

- I didn't find any poems written by my maternal grandma, Lucy Brown, but that doesn't mean that she didn't write any. There are still papers to be examined in the boxes cluttering my office, my shed, and Mom's house.

- My mom, Joan Brown Young, used to love to help us with writing assignments, especially if it involved poetry. I am including two poems she wrote, one written when the teenage son of one of my cousins died of cancer and the other after the death of an elderly woman whom she had helped as an LVN. My mom had always wanted to be a nurse, so when her ninth child was four and the rest were all in school, she went to school at one of the local hospitals to get her license to be an LVN. (Her youngest son attended "Grandma School" with her mom.) She graduated in August, passed the license exams with more than double the minimum score required, and got her LVN license in October, when she was 44 years old and had seven children still living at home. The oldest two had moved out and were on their own.

Front: Joan and her mother, Lucy Brown
Middle: 3rd great-grandma, Corinia Mack
Back: Maude Brown and her mother Jennie Webster

- Out of six boys, at least four of them have written poems. One of them was my younger brother Steve, who died in 2020. My oldest brother writes a lot of political satire, with some unique stretching of historical facts. Two other brothers have written poetry recently. Phil has allowed me to include two of his poems, one about Dad and one about Mom and a special present he received. I asked my youngest brother, Larry, to write a poem similar to mine about Steve being called to Heaven to help Dad. When Dad died, Steve had written a humorous poem explaining that Dad had been called to Heaven to help "fix" things there.

- Being a part of a large family with a fondness for writing, my husband, Jim, has written a couple of poems himself, both honoring me and wives in general. In one he compares a wife to fine crystal. In the other he says men should seek to know their wives as God does, as a beautiful treasure. That was an excellent way to win this wife's heart. I have also learned that all of his siblings have written poems and that some of his uncles wrote songs. Writing poetry is in his family history too.

- My sister Carol has also agreed to let me include a poem, which she will also be publishing in a book *JoaniPony: A Daughter's Thoughts and Memories of Her Mother with Dementia*. In her book, there are fourteen one-page stories about Mom, with my illustrations for each, as well as a longer story about all the things Mom did for her family before she got dementia. You might laugh and cry as you read it, sometimes both at the same time.

- My younger daughter, Kimberly, began writing for fun before she could actually write. At first, she drew the pictures, and I wrote the words she dictated. In kindergarten the teacher encouraged the children in her class to write stories, sounding out the words, even if they weren't spelled correctly. Kimberly took that to heart and wrote as often as she could. By the end of that year, my daughter had learned the correct spellings of many words, and over time she acquired a vast vocabulary. She still pens prose and poetry. She has allowed me to include one of the rhyming poems she wrote as a child and another that she wrote as a young adult.

- Kimberly's son, Daniel, reads more often than he writes. Most of his writing has been done for school and university assignments, but occasionally he has been inspired to write about pets, family, or science fiction, including a few stories he made up during elementary school. His family had a pet cockatiel named Max, and when he had to come up with an ode about someone for school, she became his topic. He also created the digital drawing of Max which appears with the poem.

- One of my granddaughters, who recently turned eleven, wrote a poem about our dog, Mazda, after he died. He was almost fourteen years old. I had previously encouraged her to try writing a poem, but this one was all her idea. She was only nine when she wrote it. Like the rest of our family, she likes to read and learn new things. She watches educational TV shows about the brain and other scientific topics and shows that demonstrate how to make all kinds of things.

- The love for learning runs deep in this family!

- I am ending the chapter with a poem I also wrote about my dog Mazda, but one I wrote about three years after we brought him home from the shelter. He never did much like the idea of being a dog. He felt like he was one of the people. Sometimes pets are a big part of our families. That is why I am including this poem and some photos of him. When we babysat our granddaughter as an infant, he would get frustrated with us if we didn't attend to her quickly enough when she cried. He would lick her cheek until we stopped what we were doing and picked her up. When she sat in her bouncer playing with her toys, he sometimes decided to get one of his toys and sit beside her with his own toy. If I tried to work at my computer desk, he wanted to get into my lap or chair and try to figure out what was so much more important than him. He would put his paw against my mouse pad or keyboard and stare at the monitor or turn and look at me, to make sure I saw him doing it. He loved it when my granddaughter put a pillow under his head, a blanket over him, and his toy beside him, as he lay down on the couch. He would stand beside my husband in his recliner and have a "conversation" with him, tilting his head and using inflections in his various noises, which weren't barks or growls, but were his own version of talking. If my husband was speaking loudly about something on TV, Mazda would get on "his soap box" too. The sight was hilarious. In his mind, he was one of the people.

The contributors in this chapter retain the copyrights to their poems and drawings.

'Twas on the fifth of December
I yet well remember,
As the shades of night drew on,
A barefoot little maid
Was on my weary couch laid,
To slumber until the morn.

Many years have flown fast,
And her maidenhood past,
Around her own board they now gather;
With good cheer and song,
The day and night long,
Regardless of what be the weather.

So the years will roll on,
And to all soon be gone;
Then before we life's burden lay down,
Let us lay up our treasure
In such a full measure,
That "no man shall take our crown."

There the loved ones of yore
On that bright, shining shore,
Where sorrows and death never come,
With beckoning hand,
In that beautiful land,
Are waiting to welcome us home.

Written by Grandma Mack. December 5, 1895

(I'm not sure whose life was memorialized.)

1857   1895.

1. 'Twas on the fifth of December
   I yet well remember,
   As the shades of night drew on,
   A barefoot little maid
   Was on my weary couch laid,
   To slumber until the morn.

2. Many years have flown fast,
   And her maidenhood past,
   Around her own board they now gather;
   With good cheer and song,
   She day and night long,
   Regardless of what be the weather.

3. So the years will roll on,
   And to all soon be gone;
   Then before we life's burden lay down.
   Let us lay up our treasure,
   In such a full measure,
   That "no man shall take our crown".

4. There the loved ones of yore,
   On that bright, shining shore,
   Where sorrows and death never come;
   With beckoning hand,
   In that beautiful land,
   Are waiting to welcome us home.

   Written by Grandma Mack. Dec. 5 1895

206

The Soldier and the Quilt

Beneath this puzzle quilt, of red, and blue, and white,
The weary soldier dreamt, throughout the livelong night,
Once more he heard the battle call and rushed to the fray,
Where comrades thick around him fall,
From early dawn till ends the day,

His loved and loving ones afar, with anxious heart await.
The dread report to them may bring the sealing of his fate,
Yet, in "God's land," a Soldier Home,
Received him, never more to roam;
While many loved and loyal braves
Sleep far away, in unknown graves.

C. M. Mack
(Corinia Maria Mack)
Lenox, Ohio
November, 27, 1892

(The note on the poem says, "To be sent with the Sandusky 'Tea' quilt," but I have no idea what that is all about.)

Beneath this puzzle quilt, of red, and blue, and white,
The weary soldier dreams, throughout the livelong night,
Once more he hears the battle call, and rushes to the fray,
Where comrades thick around him fall, from early dawn
                                            'till ends the day,
His loved and loving ones afar, with anxious heart
                                            await
The dread report to them may bring the sealing
                                            of his fate,
Yet, in "Gods land" a Soldier Home, receives him,
                                            never more to roam;
While many loved and loyal braves
Sleep far away, in unknown graves.

                                            CMMack
        Nov 27th 1892   Venox Ohio

To be Sent with the Sandusky
"Tea" quilt

"In memory of the dead"

Poor blind Granma has gone to rest,
In that land of heavenly bliss,
Where all the pure, the good, and blest
Forever there, to dwell in peace.

No more we hear the well-known voice—
Telling of Jesus' wondrous love,
She has gone to meet the loved ones there—
And join the angel choir above.

Her rocking chair stands empty now,
There's a vacant place around the hearth,
While she fills a place in the heavenly throng,
Where all is joy and peace and love.

And soon the fleeting years will pass.
Then we shall be called to that haven of rest,
While others here our places fill,
For such is life from year to year.

C. G. M. W.
(Corrie Geneva "Jennie" Mack Webster)

(Lucy Rolph Grover died in April of 1886, aged 86 years)

Lucy R. Grover, died April 1886
aged 86 yrs

"In memory of the dead"

Poor blind Granma has gone to rest,
In that land of heavenly bliss,
Where all the pure. the good. and blest
Forever there, to dwell in peace.

No more we hear the well known voice—
Telling of Jesus wondrous love,
She has gone to meet the loved ones
And join the angel choir above, there—

Her rocking chair stands empty now,
There's a vacant place around the hearth,
                    (space)
While she fills a place in the heavenly—
Where all is joy. and peace. and love, strong,

· · · · · — · · · · · · — · · · · · · · · — · · ·

And soon the fleeting years will pass,
Then we shall be called to that haven of
                                          rest.
While others here. our places fill,
For such is life from year to year.

C. G. M. W.

210

In Memoriam

....

Darling Katie, you have left us,
To join the heavenly band,
Where we hope someday to meet you,
In that bright and sunny land.

Why was it that you left us
While you were yet so young,
When you, dear one, were needed,
While your work was just begun?

How we miss your loving face,
And long to hear that gentle voice.
But you are gone: can time erase
The pang of Death, and we with you rejoice?

There is a bright and happy land,
Where sorrow never comes,
Where the white robed angel band
Dwell together, in that beautiful mansion—
Not made with hands.

We shall sleep but not forever.
There will be a glorious dawn.
We shall meet to part no never,
On the resurrection morn.

To Katie from Jennie
(Jennie Mack)

"In Memoriam."

1st Darling Katie you have left us,
          To join the heavenly band
     Where we hope some day to meet you,
          In that bright ed sunny land.

2nd Why was it that you left us
          While you were yet so young,
     When you, dear one, were needed,
          While your work was just begun.

3rd   How we miss your loveing face,
              And long to hear that gentle voice,
         But you are gone: can time erace
     The pang of death? Ed we with your
                              rejoice?

4th   There is a bright ed happy land,
              Where sorrow never comes,
              Where the white robed angel band
     Dwell togeathe, in that beautifull mansion
                  not made with hands.

5th   We shall sleep but not forever,
              There will be a glorious dawn,
         We shall meet to part no never,
              On the resurrection morn.

                    To Katie "from" Jennie

212

Here is a tale I would have you to know
Came straight from the fun of her granddaughter. Oh!
'Twas born 'midst confusion, the result of a doubt,
That "Ma" was not able to help Ethlyn out,
With the Santa Claus story for school the next day,
So read it through carefully. What you think of it say.

Santa's Disappointment

"Oh, dear!" exclaimed Santa, "Oh, what shall I do?
Christmas 'most here and the war not through.
My toys only started, the candy canes old
And all the material down in the hold
Of my Christmas ship, which is tied up in port,
With a row of big guns along every fort.
And no one will venture upon open sea
To sail a big ship, not even for me.

"I had planned such a Christmas of joy this time,
And now it is coming with horror and crime
To the children of foreign lands. Nay, even here.
It touches our hearts with a feeling of fear.
I have dealt out much happiness throughout my long life.
That is, I must say, with the help of my wife.
But now we are baffled, can see no way through.
So you wonder I cry, 'Oh, what shall we do?'"

"Fear not, Santa dear, here comes a great friend, indeed,
Who always is waiting to help those in need;
With wealth all unstinted, with comfort and cheer,
To gladden the hearts of the homeless this year.
'Tis our loved Uncle Sam, honored by all on earth
Who offers this aid, because of the birth
Of the Babe in the manger, who cares for us all:
The rich and the poor, the great and the small."
Oh, may this love broaden, touch all hearts and fill
The whole world with His kindness, sweet peace and good will.

M.W.B.
(Maude Webster Brown)

Here is a tale I would have you to know
Came straight from the pen of her granddaughter. &
'Twas born 'midst confusion, the result of a doubt,
That "Ma" was not able to help Ethlyn out,
With the Santa Claus story for school the next day.
So read it through carefully. What you think of it say.

Santa's Disappointment.

"Oh dear!" exclaimed Santa, "Oh, what shall I do?
Christmas 'most here and the war not through.
My toys only started, the candy canes old.
And all the material down in the hold
Of my Christmas ship, which is tied up in port,
With a row of big guns along every fort.
And no one will venture upon open sea
To sail a big ship, not even for me.

"I had planned such a Christmas of joy this time.
And now it is coming with horror and crime
To the children of foreign lands. Nay, even here
It touches our hearts with a feeling of fear.
I have dealt out much happiness throughout my long life.
That is, I must say, with the help of my wife.
But now we are baffled, can see no way through.
Do you wonder I cry, 'Oh, what shall we do?'"

"Fear not Santa, dear, here comes a great friend, indeed,
Who always is waiting to help those in need;
With wealth all unstinted, with comfort and cheer,
To gladden the hearts of the homeless this year.
'Tis our loved Uncle Sam, honored by all on earth
Who offers this aid, because of the birth
Of the Babe in the manger, who cares for us all.
The rich and the poor, the great and the small."
Oh, may this love broaden, touch all hearts and fill
The whole world with His kindness, sweet peace and good will.

(M. W. B.)

215

Billy and the Crane

Legend has it that the crane stands for peace. At last I have found peace and freedom from pain. It was hard to leave those that I love. Now, like the crane, I can soar above the clouds and once again see and know the beauty of God's world. I am happy here.

I wish to thank you with all my heart for your love, your strength, your courage, and your devotion. I couldn't have gotten through what I had to do without you. I know it was hard on you, but our love saw us through.

So now, as I soar above, I keep watch over you and I pray for you. I miss you, but then I remember all the good times, those precious memories, and it eases my heart.

One day in God's own time we will be together again, and we will soar together in all my favorite places. We will share our memories and laugh together again. Life goes on, first in this world, and then through all eternity.

When you wear this crane, remember it reminds us of peace.

Life goes on, live it, laugh again for I am always near you and share the laughter with you.

And remember I shall always love you.

Joan Young
(written for a niece after the death of her teenage son)

Motherhood

. . . .

Motherhood is eternal. Even when she crosses from time into eternity, she remains our mother. Her love and her prayers for us do not cease.

She has taught us how to live with courage, honesty, and caring. Her faith in God sustained her and now gives us the strength to go on.

A mother's love is like seeds she planted in us and they come forth in each generation. Through the memory of her, the faith and values she taught live on in us. They do not die.

Like this rose, that love blooms again and again through us. The white rose reminds us of the Blessed Virgin.

I hope you enjoy the roses and remember with joy a mother's love. She is only a prayer away.

Joan Young
(written about a deceased patient to comfort the woman's daughter)

The Patriarch

He was a quiet man,
Trustworthy and trusting,
His cars, often old, and sometimes rusting.
He drove us to school himself.
Always food on the table, and more on the shelf.
Six kids in a Beetle, going to school, felt quite like sardines in a can.

He was a brilliant man,
He'd teach you anything if you'd ask him to,
Color codes of resistors, ROYGBIV rainbow hues.
Oxide on paper to copy a voice,
On free will decisions, how to make the right choice.
Though his fan club was big, I know it's a fact, I was one of his nine biggest fans.

He was an honest man,
I learned more with my eyes than ever through hearing,
Like not telling lies, and how to be caring.
How to work hard, and how to be thrifty,
How to be kind, how not to be shifty.
The things of worth I've done in my life, he's where they all began.

He was a gentle man,
He showed how he loved us, even when we weren't near,
How to be steadfast, and how to face fear.
I learned a lot from my dad, he loved us intensely.
Now that he's gone, I will miss him immensely.
Amen.

Phil Young

The Present

. . . .

I woke up Christmas morning, and underneath the tree
was a little bitty package, who's tag said it was for me.

There was no bow or ribbon, its wrapping not the best;
the present made me curious, but I wasn't too impressed.

The name-plate said it was for me, but it didn't say from whom.
All kinds of thoughts ran through my head, my mind began to zoom.

I tore the package open, and in my mother's hand
was a wrinkled, ragged letter, nestled in a rubber band.

My mother passed away last December, but put here just for me
was the note she on her death-bed wrote, about finally getting free.

"My son, before I journeyed home, I did what you had said I should;
I asked my God's forgiveness, and He gave it, like you said He would.

"I know I was a sinner (I know you were one too.),
but I know through Jesus' precious blood, Heaven's portals I'll pass through."

All Christmas day, through teary eyes at Mom's epistle I would stare,
ever thankful of the joy that such a modest gift had shared.

He came down Christmas morning and in a manger low,
was the Lord of all creation wrapped in ragged, torn up clothes.

There were no royal courtiers, no grand parade through palace gates;
just a lowly stable and a feeding trough comprised His secular estate.

He'd no standing army, no militia to rely upon,
just an humble group of fishermen like Andrew, Peter, James, and John.

He wasn't much to look at, just a baby mild and meek
with a teen-aged mother and a working dad, sleeping with the oxen and the bleating sheep.

This little babe, on Christmas morn, laid in a manger stall
wasn't much to look at, but was the greatest gift of all.

Phil Young

Mr. Young's Assistant

Steve said Heaven wasn't quite right.
Dad was called there by the Lord
To help fix things that were aging,
So all could be restored.

The Pearly Gates were creaking
And starting to show some rust.
Even God's appliances needed repair
By a man whom He could trust.

And Dad was a whiz at mending blenders.
His TV tweak let there be light.
His knack with a trusty sewer snake
Stopped an unholy mess on Holy Night.

He fixed God's table's wobbly legs.
Now it's stable where it stands.
Yep, Dad fixed most everything in Heaven,
But he needed some extra hands.

So the good Lord looked over all His lists.
He had a few billion to pick from,
But He was choosing Dad's new right hand this time;
He had to apply His wisdom.

In the end, God sought Dad's counsel,
And the answer was: "Well, let's see. . .
You'll want someone handy, honest, hardworking,
And humble and witty — you know. . . like me."

Now the Lord'll have a worthy new helper.
Up there in the garage with Dad,
And probably thinking up another good tale to tell
While we're all down here, sad.

Larry Young

(This poem was written in response to my poem about our brother Steve being called
to Heaven to help our dad. Steve had written a poem after Dad died talking about how
Dad was called to Heaven to help God fix the things starting to wear out. Of course,
things don't actually wear out there. These were but futile (and humorous) attempts to
explain why these two good men had to leave us. They are still missed.)

A Wife Is Like Fine Crystal

A wife is like fine crystal,
Delicate to the touch;
Shines when treated properly;
Breaks easily, but at times is surprisingly tough;
Sensitive to harsh, loud, or shrill sounds;
Beautiful to look at;
Sings when touched in the right way;
Sparkles under the light;
Is in high demand;
Needed most for special occasions;
Works best when the spirit is allowed to breathe;
Very elegant when held lightly;
Will last a lifetime if handled with great care.

You husbands likewise, live with your wives in an
understanding way, as with a weaker vessel, since
she is a woman; and grant her honor as a fellow heir
of the grace of life, so that your prayers may not be hindered.
I Peter 3:7

Jim Goza

The Hidden Treasure

A good wife is a treasure, the Bible says,
Though some shall never find.
Until the Spirit of Christ indwells,
Man's search can be unkind.
The Word of God is a map to share.
"At the cross thou shalt find."
When men are willing to die to self,
Will her radiance begin to shine.

A wife of noble character who can find?
She is worth far more than rubies.
Proverbs 31:10

Husbands, love your wives, just as Christ loved
the church and gave himself up for her... to
present her to himself as a radiant church... holy
and blameless....
Ephesians 5:25, 27

Jim Goza

Momma,

I loved you when I was little,
    And you taught me things.

I loved you when I was young,
    And you disciplined me.

I loved you when I was a teenager,
    And I thought I hated you.

I loved you as we got older,
    And I had to help you with things.

And I will love you still,
    After you don't remember me.

Carol Young Moreno

(for her book, *JoaniPony: A Daughter's Thoughts and Memories of Her Mother with Dementia*)

A Mother's the Best Friend a Daughter Can Have

A mother's the best friend a daughter can have.
For she's sweet and understanding
And neat and not demanding.
She's gentle and kind
And has a calm mind.
She listens to what you say
And wipes your tears away.
She cheers you up when you're sad
And almost never gets mad.
No friend understands you more
Than your mother, that's for sure.
She knows what you need,
So you don't have to plead.
She is all of joy and love,
Sent down here from up above.
A mother's the best friend a daughter can have.

Kimberly (Kimi) Taylor
(written when she was 10 years old)

Mother

My mother always knew
Just how to make things right:
When I was black and blue,
Or when I was filled with fright,
She would say, "I love you,"
Pull me close, and hold me tight.
Then my troubles would seem few,
And my burdens would seem light.

Even as I grew,
And I passed my mom in height,
When troubles would ensue,
She'd help me in my plight.
She knew just what to do,
And she was usually right.
Mother taught me what is true.
And her love shines like a light.

Kimberly Kuchar
(written as a young adult)

Ode to Max

Max is a little bird
Who likes to chirp and tweet.
Sometimes she acts absurd,
And sometimes she is sweet.

She's not great at flying,
Though she tries her heart out.
On our hands she starts flapping
And gets a good workout.

When excited she starts to dance
And chirp a pretty beat.
Depending on the circumstance,
We may give her a treat.

She loves it when I pet her.
She gives sweet kisses too.
I never will forget her.
Maxine, I love you.

Daniel Kuchar
(written for a school assignment)

Max by Daniel Kuchar

Mazda

Mazda was a silly one;
He loved to play and bark.
He loved to snuggle his family,
But didn't like the dark.

Mazda was intelligent.
He'd bark so Dad would see
Him raise his leg to go out,
'Cuz he really had to pee.

Whenever we ate our food,
He wanted his share too.
If we threw his toys down the hall,
He'd pick them up and chew.

When Kaelyn was a little girl,
He loved to lick her face.
He was a curious little dog
Who loved to run and race.

Kaelyn Davis
(written shortly after Mazda died)

Mazda, Our New "Little Boy"

Mazda is a sweet little "boy."
He's funny and cute and brings such joy.
He likes to run out in the yard,
But catching him is very hard.

He tries to escape in the neighborhood.
It's just too hard to always be good.
He shadows his "mom" wherever she goes
And barks at anyone he doesn't know.

He loves to go in the car for a ride.
When he "messes" the carpet, he knows where to hide.
He talks to his "dad" by the side of his chair,
And wants to go with us everywhere.

He loves to snuggle with "Mom" and "Dad."
He's the sweetest dog we've ever had.

Robin Goza

(This was written several years after we got him from a shelter in 2008. When Kaelyn wrote the poem after he died in 2022, I decided to look for the poem I had written years before. He was smart and funny and never seemed to realize that he wasn't one of the people in the family. I have no doubt that many of the readers have a dog or know of one like Mazda, who is convinced he or she truly is "People.")

Printed in the United States
by Baker & Taylor Publisher Services